THE BEST
MIDWEST
RESTAURANT
COOKING

THE BEST MIDWEST RESTAURANT COOKING

by Margaret E. Guthrie

with the assistance of Annie L. Saart

and a Foreword by Louis I. Szathmáry

IOWA STATE UNIVERSITY PRESS / AMES

Manufactured in the United States of America

♾ This book is printed on acid-free paper.

First edition, 1989

Book design by Joanne E. Kinney

Library of Congress Cataloging-in-Publication Data

Guthrie, Margaret E.
    The best Midwest restaurant cooking / by Margaret E. Guthrie.—1st
ed.
        p.   cm.
    Includes bibliographical references.
    ISBN 0–8138–0663–1
    1. Cookery—Middle West. I. Title.
TX715.G986   1989
641.5′0977—dc20   89–20189
                                                                   CIP

To the memory of
Etta Thomas and Rose Dias,
two women who taught me that
respect for what you're going
to eat has to come first

Contents

Foreword

When I arrived, a "greenhorn" from Europe, in 1961, I did what most European immigrants did—settled as close to the Atlantic shore as one could.

Some years passed, and I couldn't get used to the tempo and mood of life in New York. They were too fast and too impersonal for me.

My first trip to the Deep South, with the idea of taking a job and settling there, made me realize that my biological clock, adjusted to a certain tempo in Europe, was too fast for the southern lifestyle.

Oregon and California were also running at different speeds than I. But when I came to Chicago, I knew, yes—I just knew the first day after I arrived—that this was the place for me.

I became a midwesterner faster than I thought possible. I wasn't only acclimatized, I was also spoiled. Here, I was only half as far from everything as before. More than a quarter of a century ago, when I opened The Bakery in Chicago, I realized that I could obtain absolutely everything I wanted—lobster from Maine, caribou from Canada, Olympia oysters from Portland, freshly picked dates from the Nevada plantations, artichokes from California, blue corn from New Mexico, stone crabs from Florida, oysters from Chesapeake Bay, plus all the native richness of the Midwest.

While I had the impression that New York was basically the westernmost colony of Europe and California the easternmost playground of Hawaii, Chicago was and is to me the most American of cities.

Where else could you have within walking distance on public display a major work of Picasso, Miro, Chagall, and Calder in the shadow of buildings designed by Louis Sullivan and Mies van der Rohe?

If you know Midwest restaurant history, you know that it is long, with proud traditions. The first directory of a fledgling Chicago listed several public waiters who were available for hire for large parties by restaurants, banquet halls, coffee houses, and private families.

Ethnic restaurants are not new to Chicago. At the turn of the century, a Chinese restaurant in downtown Chicago seated six hundred in its main dining room. At one time, more than a dozen Hungarian restaurants existed on North Avenue around Sedgwick and Halstead. These are only two of the ethnic groups, and everybody knows about the Polish, Scandinavian, and German restaurants.

Now is the time to prepare for the twenty-first century. We have only a decade to get there. From this book we can learn much about our present based on the experience of the past. Nothing prepares us as well for tomorrow as what we know about yesterday and today.

Louis I. Szathmáry
Former owner, The Bakery, Chicago, Illinois
Chef Laureate, Johnson and Wales University, Providence, Rhode Island

 # Acknowledgments

First, nothing I do would be possible without the small circle of devoted friends and family who put up with me: Judy Borree, Judy Miller, Annie Topham, and Martha Fineman. My three children, Cort, Katie, and Annie, who maintain my sense of humor, and finally, friend and counselor Michael Davis.

Special thanks on this project go to Karen Odessa Piper, Stephen Langlois, and Louis Szathmáry. And to the staff of the Iowa State University Press for their immense enthusiasm and cooperation.

Above all, though, this book would not be possible if it were not for the work of all those chefs and cooks out there who responded so enthusiastically to my idea. This book is really for them, so there's something more than a stack of empty, dirty dishes to show for their dedication to good food.

 *Introduction*

I t all began with Wisconsin, where I now live, and a job I held as associate editor in a small regional publishing house in 1983. The editor-in-chief, Mark LeFebvre, asked me to develop some potential publishing projects.

One of the ideas I came up with was *The Best Recipes of Wisconsin Inns and Restaurants.* It seemed to me that there was plenty of good food available in Wisconsin restaurants, that there were innovative and interesting things happening in the restaurant business, and that there was a healthy tourism industry here. Also, no one had done anything similar.

While LeFebvre liked the idea, for other reasons it wasn't possible to do the book with Stanton & Lee. Being a generous man, Mark told me to consider the idea my property. I did and promptly approached a friend, Charles Spanbauer at Amherst Press. He thought it was a great idea and so I began eating my way across Wisconsin, collecting recipes as I went.

The Wisconsin book sold so well that we went on to do Minnesota, Michigan, Ohio, and Illinois outside of the Chicago city limits. It took three years to eat my way across a major portion of the Midwest, chronicling my discoveries as I traveled. It was one of the most interesting and enjoyable journeys I have ever made. Not only did I learn a great deal about the region's food, but I experienced the kind of hospitality I thought had disappeared, and I was greeted with enthusiasm and interest by every chef, restaurant owner, and manager with whom I spoke. I also ate extremely well, sometimes as often as five times a day.

Perhaps the most important thing I learned in my travels is that the Midwest is much underrated as a place to eat. There is wonderful food everywhere in the Midwest, if you know where to look, and I think there is as much excitement and innovation in the restaurant trade here as there is anywhere.

First, the Midwest encompasses a vast region geographically. Within that region we grow everything from cranberries to persimmons, peaches to pecans. We harvest morels and wild rice. Small farmers are beginning to grow specialty produce and raise game for the restaurant trade, gourmet food shops, and farmers' markets that are springing up everywhere. Oriental vegetables, radicchio, broccoli rabe, and other vegetables that no one had heard of ten years ago are now easily found near the metropolitan centers of the Midwest. No one looks at you as though you are mad when you ask about edible flowers and oak leaf lettuce.

We can't be beaten when it comes to the things we've always done well like cheese, pork, bacon and hams, sausages, duckling, veal and beef. Iowa *and* Indiana both claim the world's best popcorn. We even have a cultivated butter, made as it's made in Switzerland.

The native foods like cranberries, maple syrup, wild rice, pumpkin, pecans, and blueberries have become integrated into the cuisines, the recipes brought over from the old country by the waves of immigrants who settled the Midwest. The ethnic mix in the Midwest is the richest anywhere in this country, perhaps because of the land—some of the richest, most productive soil in the world—perhaps just because the region is so large. For whatever reason, the Midwest has enjoyed large influxes of French, Germans, Dutch, Swedes, Norwegians, Danes, Poles, Italians, Scots, Irish, even southern African-Americans and New England Yankees. As each wave settled, it incorporated the new foods into its cooking and so began moving toward a new cuisine or style of cooking, using the old ways and incorporating the new foods.

The recipes brought from the old country to the new began to evolve from their origins and over time developed into American or midwestern recipes and foods. The evolving was aided by the new foods available and by the ethnic mixture that took place here, as well as new circumstances, climate, and geography.

Today, Southeast Asians are bringing their spices and seasonings to the Midwest and beginning to influence the food here. One of the highest concentrations of Southeast Asian restaurants occurs in the Minneapolis–St. Paul area. There are over a hundred restaurants serving various Southeast Asian cuisines in the metropolitan area. Other area restaurateurs have begun using lemongrass, fresh ginger, and the other spices and seasonings brought by this new wave of immigrants.

Since the availability of local foodstuffs still influences what we eat, the Midwest has yet to develop an overall cuisine, a style or manner of cooking. The all-you-can-eat Friday night fish fry is a tradition in the Great Lakes areas of Michigan, Wisconsin, and Minnesota. If you want a tenderloin sandwich you will go someplace like the cafe in Anamosa, Iowa. And you won't say you want the *pork* tenderloin sandwich because they'll look at you as though you had two heads. There is no other tenderloin in Anamosa, Iowa.

Go to Bayfield, Wisconsin, for whitefish livers, eat them in several places, and decide who does them best. Go to Council Grove, Kansas, to the Hays House for barbecue. Along the Mississippi you can find places that still serve catfish cheeks. No, it's not the local version of a snipe hunt—old-timers will tell you it's the best part of the catfish.

The climate varies so widely in this region that inevitably certain things only grow in certain places. Cranberries only grow in Wisconsin, and Missouri has wild pecans and is the world's largest supplier of black walnuts. Michigan grows peaches, and Ohio and Wisconsin are major maple syrup producers. Wild rice is big in Minnesota and Wisconsin. Michigan and Wisconsin are the morel states. Iowa is the place for pheasant as well as pork and popcorn. Ohio grows more tomatoes. Indiana does ducklings as succulent and tasty as any from Long Island ever were. Apples are a major crop in several states.

As a result you will find a near-perfect Cream of Wild Rice Soup at Jax Cafe in Minneapolis; a terrific Morel and Beer Bread at Tapawingo in Ellsworth, Michigan; great Cranberry Muffins at North Star Lodge in Star Lake, Wisconsin. The Golden Lamb Inn in Lebanon, Ohio, has been serving world-class apple pie for over a hundred years and to ten of our presidents.

Cooking in the Midwest is, like the cuisines of Italy and Morocco, a home-based cuisine. In both those countries the best cooking has been and continues to be done in the home by women. That was certainly true of the Midwest as it emerged as the nation's breadbasket. Some of the finest cooking continues to be done here in homes. I still remember the tantalizing descriptions in an article published in *Gourmet* magazine several years ago by a woman who wrote of helping her mother with the meals put on the table for the haying and threshing crews. Recently, I worked with Judith Dunbar Hines, who grew up on a farm in southern Illinois, and her description of the Jersey cream, the fresh eggs, the flavorful chicken, and the juicy strawberries and sweet corn from the family garden was similarly mouthwatering.

In a conversation with the late Bert Greene, noted cookbook author and food columnist, in March of 1988, we agreed that there are probably as many recipes for fried chicken in the Midwest as there are people cooking it. He said it was one of the things he collected on his trips—recipes for fried chicken.

Some of this cooking migrates naturally into the restaurant business as it has at the White Way in Durant, Iowa, where Carroll Marshall "tinkered" with his mother's recipe for Raisin Cream Pie. Or at the Swedish Pantry in Escanaba, Michigan, where Betty Mycunich uses recipes of her mother's. Lucile Killeen's Potato Doughnuts is a recipe that Judy Killeen-Sarkozy's mother devised after a trip to Chicago and dinner in an elegant hotel, which refused her the recipe for their potato rolls. The hotel is defunct but you can get Lucile's doughnuts at Sarkozy's Bakery & Cafe in Kalamazoo, Michigan. At Quivey's Grove outside Madison, Wisconsin, head chef Craig Kuenning has put Chocolate Steamed Pudding with Ellie's Mom's Sauce on the menu. "Ellie's Mom" is Craig's grandmother and her Chocolate Steamed Pudding and Sauce is a dessert "to die for."

Much of this originally home-based cuisine has been adapted and enhanced by chefs like Harlan Peterson of Tapawingo with his Apple Cider Tart and Stephen Langlois of Prairie with his Warm Persimmon Pudding with Dried Blueberries. These are dishes that your mother or grandmother might have made, if they had had the culinary knowledge these chefs have.

Besides the ethnic influences that have come to bear and the effects of climate and soil on what will grow where, the most important current influence is the arrival of young, enthusiastic chefs in the Midwest. They are following in the footsteps of such pioneers as Louis Szathmáry in Chicago, Richard Perry in St. Louis, and Michael Comisar in Cincinnati. Some, from here originally, left to train and work in Europe, the East Coast, and California. They are returning with enthusiasm and newly acquired skills, eager to utilize the Midwest's vast array of foods. One chef compared what is available to him in the north central region of the Midwest to the foods available in Normandy, France.

A friend recently remarked to me over lunch that we seem to have gone from a vogue for baby vegetables to one for baby chefs, referring to the extreme youthfulness of some of the most important chefs now changing the taste of midwestern diners. This youthful infusion has meant an ever-expanding horizon for the region's restaurants, food, and cuisine.

In addition to new, young American chefs are European chefs who want to own their own restaurants and who prefer the relatively uncrowded field here in the Midwest. Men like Dieter Krug of L'Auberge in Dayton, Ohio, or Pierre Pollin of Le Titi de Paris, Arlington Heights, Illinois.

Another positive development, which may have far-reaching effects on our agriculture, is the contracting by many of the chefs and restaurants with individual farmers and producers to obtain local specialty products directly. Many small farmers now are finding that the way to survive is to grow radicchio and arugula rather than, or as well as, corn and soybeans. Buffalo, elk, venison, pheasant, and quail are now appearing on regional menus. These are native foods, with the exception of pheasant, a successful transplant, and are now being reintroduced to enthusiastic diners. Rainbow trout and catfish are being farmed successfully and supplied to both restaurants and home consumers. Farmers' markets are enjoying a healthy resurgence as midwestern palates become more attuned to eating what's fresh and local, rather than what's been shipped over long distances, gassed on the way to induce ripeness, and wrapped in styrofoam and plastic film so you can neither touch it, smell it, nor really see it. Farmers are finding that venison may be more profitable than beef. One Wisconsin dairy farmer is successfully raising snails for area restaurants. Farmers are finding a ready-made market for what they grow in area restaurants and gourmet food shops. When consumer demand increases, many of these products will become readily available everywhere.

The Farmers' Home Hotel in Galena, Illinois, contracts with a local farmer for free-range and organically fed pigs. They smoke their own hams and bacons and advertise the fact on their menu. Sammy's in Cleveland, Ohio, helped two or three farmers set up greenhouses so the restaurant would be assured of a reliable, year-round supply of specialty produce.

In a sense the Midwest is returning to its beginnings. Local farmhouse cheeses; eggs from organically fed and free-ranging hens; free-range chickens; and pork, beef, veal, and lamb raised without benefit of steroids, hormones, and antibiotics are now being regularly supplied to some midwestern restaurants by individual farmers. Fresh herbs and more exotic produce like white tomatoes, edible flowers, and European and Oriental vegetables are now being commonly grown throughout the Midwest because there is a demand for them.

As the public's palate is educated by these efforts, we will all benefit. The result may well be that in ten or fifteen years the Midwest will have developed an overall, unified cuisine—a style or manner of cooking, as the *Random House Dictionary* puts it. Right now, the Midwest is in a fascinating state of development that makes traveling and eating your way through the states, as I have done, a marvelous experience, one which I hope to continue to enjoy. When you try some of these recipes, when you try some of the restaurants that so generously contributed to this book, I think you will agree that the Midwest can hold its own with restaurants anywhere.

A NOTE OR TWO ABOUT THE RECIPES

First, if your favorite restaurant is missing from these pages, please remember this book is the result of a one-woman odyssey and I may have missed a few. Also, a few restaurants contacted chose not to be in the book.

Next and most important, some of the chefs who contributed to this book have made a request. They ask that you read any recipe you intend to try all the way through at least once and that you be sure you have all ingredients before you begin. Most important of all, do NOT substitute ingredients.

One chef told me of a woman who accused him of leaving out a secret ingredient so that she would be unable to duplicate his recipe. When leading her through the recipe, she announced calmly that she had substituted canned spinach for fresh. Use the ingredients specified if you want the dish to turn out.

When reading the recipes, flour means all-purpose white, unless otherwise specified. Sugar means granulated white, butter means regular table butter, eggs are large. Good cooking and good eating!

THE BEST
MIDWEST
RESTAURANT
COOKING

BRUNCH

As you might guess the word *brunch* evolved from the words *breakfast* and *lunch*. It did so between 1895 and 1900, so the custom has been with us for some time.

It has lately enjoyed a renewed popularity, probably because it is such a relaxed and enjoyable way to entertain. As more and more women work full-time, entertaining guests on the weekend has become almost a necessity, if it's to be done at home. And that's where brunch has come into its own.

Midwestern cooks and chefs offer fare at both ends of the spectrum. This section begins with breakfast dishes like hotcakes and waffles and ends with some terrific casseroles.

Apple Fritters

2 cups flour
½ cup confectioner's sugar
2 teaspoons baking powder
2 eggs, slightly beaten
½ cup milk
2 medium apples, cored and
    chopped, peel left on

Mix together all the dry ingredients. Add the eggs and milk. Add the fruit and mix well. Drop off a soup spoon into hot fat (about 375 degrees) and fry about 2 minutes on a side. Roll in confectioner's sugar and serve hot with maple syrup.

Yields about 24 fritters

Betsey Mills Dining Room
300 4th Street
Marietta, Ohio

Minnesota Wild Rice Waffles

Innkeeper Mary Martin made up this recipe by taking a basic waffle recipe and "adding things that sounded right."

3 eggs, separated
1½ cups milk
1¾ cups flour, sifted
4 teaspoons baking powder
½ teaspoon salt
¼ pound margarine, melted
1 cup or more cooked wild rice

Beat the egg yolks with a wire whisk. Stir in the milk, sifted flour, baking powder, salt, and melted margarine. Mix until smooth. Add in the wild rice and mix thoroughly.

Preheat the waffle iron. Beat the egg whites until they form stiff peaks. Carefully fold them into the batter. Bake in the preheated waffle iron and serve with pure maple syrup.

Yields 3 large waffles, 12 quarters

The Canterbury Inn
723 Second Street, S.W.
Rochester, Minnesota

Sunday Cinnamon Rolls

Technically, these rolls should be in the chapter devoted to baked goods, but they seem a terrific choice for a Sunday brunch. Cinnamon rolls are one of the latest "in" foods. Most of us never knew they were "out."

1 package dry yeast
1/4 cup warm water (110 to 115 degrees)
1 cup milk, scalded
2 tablespoons sugar
2 tablespoons butter
1 teaspoon salt
3 1/2 cups sifted flour
1 egg

FILLING
1/2 cup brown sugar
1/4 cup melted butter
1 1/2 teaspoons cinnamon

TOPPING
1/2 cup light or dark corn syrup
1/4 cup brown sugar
1/4 cup melted butter
1/2 teaspoon cinnamon

Soften the yeast in the warm water. Combine the scalded milk, sugar, butter, and salt, mixing well and cooling to lukewarm. Add 1 cup of the sifted flour and beat well. Beat in the softened yeast and egg. Gradually add the remaining flour to form a soft dough.

Place the dough in a greased bowl, turning to coat the dough. Cover with a clean towel and let rise in a warm place until double in bulk. Preheat the oven to 350 degrees. Butter a large baking pan. Punch down the risen dough and turn out on a lightly floured surface. Divide the dough in half. Roll out each half in a 16 × 8–inch rectangular shape. Spread the surface with filling. Roll lengthwise. Seal the edge and cut in 1-inch slices.

Mix together the topping ingredients and place in the well-greased pan. Place the roll slices cut side down in the pan on the topping. Let rise until double in bulk.

Bake in the oven until golden brown, about 20 to 25 minutes. While still warm, turn the pan upside down on a baking tray so the topping may run down the sides of the rolls. Serve warm. They may be cooled or frozen and reheated in the oven or in a microwave.

Hulbert's Restaurant
1033 Bridge Street
Ashtabula, Ohio

Banana and Walnut Hotcakes

1 cup whole wheat flour
1 cup flour
¼ cup wheat germ
⅙ cup sugar
2 teaspoons baking powder
1 teaspoon salt
1 teaspoon baking soda
2 eggs
2 cups buttermilk
¼ cup vegetable oil
¼ cup chopped walnuts
2 ripe bananas, cut into small
   pieces
Yogurt, maple syrup, and
   cinnamon (optional)

Set the grill at 375 degrees and grease with oil. Mix together all the dry ingredients. Mix together all the wet ingredients, beating well to mix thoroughly. Add the wet ingredients to the dry, stirring to mix well. Add the chopped walnuts and bananas. Measure ¼ cup of batter for each hotcake. Turn the cakes when the top is bubbly. Top the hotcakes with butter, maple syrup, or yogurt-cinnamon topping made by adding maple syrup and cinnamon to vanilla yogurt.
   Yields 1 dozen hotcakes

The Story Inn
State Highway 135 South
Nashville, Indiana

Gingerbread Waffles

2 eggs
⅓ cup sugar
½ cup molasses
6 tablespoons shortening
½ cup hot water
2 cups flour
1 teaspoon ginger
1 teaspoon baking soda
1 teaspoon cinnamon
½ teaspoon salt

Beat the eggs until they are light and lemon-colored. Add the sugar and beat again. Add the molasses and beat. Melt the shortening in the hot water.
   Sift together the dry ingredients. Preheat the waffle iron. Add the shortening mixture to the egg mixture alternately with the sifted dry ingredients. Beat thoroughly.
   Bake on the preheated waffle iron. Serve with whipped cream and bananas, Apple Cider Sauce (see the recipe in Sauces, Seasonings, and Specialties), warm applesauce, or lemon curd.

The Apple Orchard Inn
Missouri Valley, Iowa

Michigan Cassoulet

This dish is a midwestern adaptation of a traditional French casserole. The best of both worlds!

⅓ pound Michigan navy beans
1 quart rich duck or chicken
  stock
1 cup diced onion
2 cloves garlic, minced
1 ham hock
1 pound pork shoulder, diced
½ pound venison sausage,
  sliced
½ pound smoked turkey, diced
½ pound morels, cleaned
½ cup tomato sauce
Salt, pepper, and thyme to taste
Bread crumbs, buttered

Rinse and soak the beans overnight. On the following day, drain the beans. In a large pot, bring the stock to a simmer with the beans. Add the ham hock, garlic, and onions. Simmer this for about an hour. Drain the beans and return the liquid to the stove and reduce to about 1 cup.

Preheat the oven to 350 degrees. Meanwhile saute the pork and venison sausage until the meat is brown and the fat is rendered. Drain the excess fat from the pan. Now add to the pan the reduced stock, tomato sauce, beans, and meats, including the cooked meat from the ham hock. Add the rest of the ingredients. Season with salt, pepper, and thyme and simmer for about 15 minutes. Layer the mixture into individual casseroles and sprinkle the tops with buttered bread crumbs. Bake for about an hour.

The Rowe Inn
County Road C48
Ellsworth, Michigan

Harvest Casserole

This is a good brunch dish and a great way to use up garden overproduction as well.

2 medium eggplants, peeled and
   diced
4 medium zucchini, sliced
4 teaspoons salt
2 pounds hamburger
3 tomatoes, chopped
2 green peppers, chopped
2 medium onions, chopped
4 ears sweet corn, cut off the
   cob
1½ cups cooked rice
3 tablespoons chopped parsley
¼ teaspoon pepper
½ cup butter, melted
2 cups Parmesan cheese, freshly
   grated

Place the eggplant and zucchini in a colander. Sprinkle with 2 teaspoons of the salt. Let stand for 30 minutes to drain. Preheat the oven to 375 degrees.

Saute the hamburger in a skillet until the redness is gone and drain. In a large bowl, combine the hamburger, eggplant, zucchini, remaining vegetables, rice, and parsley. Sprinkle with the remaining 2 teaspoons of salt and the pepper. Place in a buttered baking dish and pour the melted butter over all. Cover and bake 45 minutes in the preheated oven. Uncover, sprinkle the Parmesan cheese on top, and bake until the vegetables are tender and the cheese is melted, about 10 minutes longer.

Yields 10 to 12 servings

The Ronneburg
Amana, Iowa

Crustless Spinach Quiche

5 ounces frozen chopped
   spinach, thawed
3 green onions, thinly sliced
⅔ cup grated Swiss cheese
⅔ cup grated cheddar cheese
9 eggs
1½ cups half and half
½ teaspoon salt
½ teaspoon pepper
Pinch each of nutmeg and garlic
   powder
Parmesan cheese to taste

Liberally butter a quiche dish. Preheat the oven to 350 degrees. Squeeze the excess moisture out of the thawed spinach. Place the vegetables and the Swiss and cheddar cheeses in the quiche dish. Lightly beat together the eggs, cream, salt, pepper, and spices. Pour over the vegetables and the cheese. Bake for 30 minutes. Remove from the oven, sprinkle Parmesan cheese on top, and return to the oven for 15 minutes more.

The Inn at Cedar Crossing
336 Louisiana Street
Sturgeon Bay, Wisconsin

Pasta Carbonara

J asper says, "As for the story of Carbonara: In the late 1800s, the coal miners in Italy would eat breakfast outside, cooking this dish in large black skillets. They would use *pancetta* and eggs and mix it with pasta."

¼ pound linguini, cooked
1 ounce olive oil
¼ onion, finely diced
4 ounces pancetta (bacon)
4 ounces prosciutto
1 egg yolk
1 egg
¼ ounce sherry
Salt and pepper
Fresh chopped parsley

Cook the linguini according to package directions and reserve.

Saute the onion, *pancetta*, and prosciutto in the olive oil until the onion is translucent. Remove from the fire and add the pasta. Toss well. Place the mixture in another pan and add the eggs and sherry. Return the pan to the stove and stir the mixture well to coat evenly with egg. Remove from the heat, season to taste with salt and pepper and sprinkle with the parsley.

It is important to remove this pasta dish from the heat immediately after adding and mixing in the eggs to avoid overcooking them.

Jasper's Italian Restaurant
408 West 75th Street
Kansas City, Missouri

Vegetarian Stuffed Peppers with Fresh Tomato Sauce

6 large bell peppers (green, red, yellow, or a combination)

3 cups cooked brown rice

3 tablespoons chopped onion

2 tablespoons chopped garlic

¼ cup olive oil

½ cup very hearty whole wheat bread crumbs

1 teaspoon capers, rinsed and drained

2 tablespoons raisins, plumped in hot water and drained

8 imported black olives, pitted, rinsed, and chopped (do not use California olives)

½ cup chopped walnuts

2 tablespoons chopped fresh sweet basil or 2 teaspoons dry basil

¼ cup fresh parsley, chopped (do not use dried flakes)

1 teaspoon orange zest, finely chopped

½ cup orange juice

1 egg

Salt (optional)

Fresh Tomato Sauce (see the following recipe)

Blanch the peppers in boiling water or microwave them to tenderize (they should still be somewhat firm). Cut the peppers in half lengthwise, leaving the stem intact. Remove the seeds and membranes. Set aside.

Preheat the oven to 350 degrees. Saute the onions and garlic in the olive oil until translucent. Combine the onion-garlic mixture with the rice, bread crumbs, capers, raisins, olives, walnuts, sweet basil, parsley, and orange zest. Mix the egg with the orange juice and toss with the filling. Taste for salt—olives and capers are both salty and, depending on your palate, additional salt may be unnecessary.

Mound the filling in the pepper halves and place the halves filling side up in a baking dish. Put ½ cup of water in the dish and cover with a lid or with aluminum foil. Bake for 45 minutes in the preheated oven. Serve with the tomato sauce.

Yields 6 servings

Pam Sherman's Bakery & Cafe
2914 Hennepin Avenue
Minneapolis, Minnesota

Fresh Tomato Sauce

1 pound fresh tomatoes, peeled
   and seeded or 1 cup canned
   tomatoes and juice
⅓ cup chopped carrot
⅓ cup chopped celery
⅓ cup chopped onion
¼ teaspoon sugar
⅓ cup olive oil

Seed the tomatoes and reserve all juices. If using fresh tomatoes, cook them in a covered saucepan for 10 minutes over medium heat. If using canned tomatoes, eliminate this step.

Add all the other ingredients and cook at a steady simmer for 30 minutes, uncovered. Coarsely puree the mixture through a food mill or in a blender. Do not make the mixture homogenous—you should be able to detect bits of the various vegetables. Return to the heat for another 15 minutes. Taste for salt.

Pam Sherman's Bakery & Cafe
2914 Hennepin Avenue
Minneapolis, Minnesota

BREADS, ROLLS, AND MUFFINS

Bread and its surrogates—rolls, muffins, scones, and biscuits—have been taken for granted in this country for far too long. For a time we uncomplainingly ate pasty, white bread, whose flour had to be reinforced with all the good things that had been milled out of it. We were told, among other things, that this bread would build strong bodies twelve ways—the most important of which was sideways, a direction not particularly healthy or attractive for the human body.

Now we are getting back to good bread, bread made the way it was meant to taste and feel and look. Bread with real texture and flavor, with a crust that must be chewed. Breads, rolls, muffins, scones, and biscuits worthy of accompanying the other foods in this book, or of being eaten on their own for their own flavor and nourishment.

And you will find on these pages bread that utilizes ingredients that grow locally, ingredients for which the Midwest is well known as well as those for which it is less known. You will find everything from morels to persimmons incorporated in bread and dried cherries to sweet potatoes in the biscuits and scones. And you will find all of them delicious.

Ozark Persimmon Bread

This bread contains persimmons and black walnuts, both indigenous products of the Missouri soil and climate.

1 cup pureed persimmons
1 teaspoon baking soda
12 tablespoons butter, room
* temperature*
1¼ cups sugar
2 eggs
1 ⅓ cups flour
½ teaspoon salt
1 teaspoon cinnamon
1 teaspoon vanilla extract
2 teaspoons lemon juice
2 tablespoons bourbon
1 cup black walnuts, chopped
¾ cup raisins

Preheat the oven to 325 degrees. Grease 2 small loaf pans.

Stir the baking soda into the persimmon puree. Set aside. Cream together the butter and sugar until smooth. Add the eggs and beat well.

Add the flour, salt, and cinnamon, along with the persimmon mixture, and beat until blended. Add the vanilla, lemon juice, and bourbon. Stir in the walnuts and raisins.

Fill the bread pans two-thirds full. Bake 45 to 60 minutes or until a toothpick inserted in the center comes out clean. Cool for 10 minutes and remove from the pans.

Yields 2 loaves

Walnut Street Bed and Breakfast
900 East Walnut Street
Springfield, Missouri

Fresh Rhubarb Bread

Innkeeper Terry Wulf makes this bread from rhubarb she purchases at the local farmers' market, a block away from the inn.

2½ cups flour
½ cup chopped pecans or
  walnuts
1 teaspoon baking powder
½ teaspoon salt
¼ teaspoon nutmeg
1 teaspoon baking soda
1¼ cups buttermilk
½ cup vegetable oil
1 egg
1 cup brown sugar
2 teaspoons vanilla extract
1½ cups coarsely chopped
  rhubarb

Preheat the oven to 350 degrees. Grease 2 loaf pans.

Mix the flour, nuts, baking powder, salt, and nutmeg in a large mixing bowl. Dissolve the baking soda in the buttermilk. Beat together the buttermilk, egg, oil, brown sugar, and vanilla.

Stir the buttermilk mixture into the dry ingredients until just moistened. The batter will be lumpy. Fold in the rhubarb. Bake for 45 to 50 minutes or until golden brown on top.

The Inn at Cedar Crossing
336 Louisiana Street
Sturgeon Bay, Wisconsin

Cherry and Pecan Bread

1 egg
6 ounces tart cherries, chopped
  and drained
1 cup sugar
½ teaspoon grated lemon rind
2 tablespoons melted butter
½ cup cherry juice
¼ cup orange juice
2 cups flour
3 teaspoons baking powder
¼ teaspoon baking soda
1 teaspoon salt
1 cup pecans, chopped

Preheat the oven to 350 degrees. Grease 2 9 × 4–inch loaf pans.

Chop the cherries, reserving the juice. In a large bowl beat the egg and then add the cherries. Stir in the sugar, lemon rind, and melted butter. Pour in the juices. Sift the flour, baking powder, baking soda, and salt together. Add this to the cherry liquid a spoonful at a time, blending thoroughly. Add the pecans. Fill the loaf pans two-thirds full. Bake for 1¼ hours until a toothpick inserted in the center comes out clean.

Yields 2 loaves

The Washington House Inn
W62 N573 Washington Avenue
Cedarburg, Wisconsin

Orange Nut Bread

This recipe for Orange Nut Bread is from the innkeeper's grandmother, Clara Childs. She made the bread every Sunday, when her family had dinner with her. It's in her honor this is served to the guests each morning. Since there are three large old pecan trees in their yard, the innkeepers use pecans in the recipe, but other nuts would work as well.

2½ cups flour
3 teaspoons baking powder
1 teaspoon salt
1 cup sugar
¼ cup butter
¾ cup milk
¼ cup freshly squeezed orange
   juice
1 egg
3 tablespoons freshly grated
   orange rind
1 cup chopped pecans

Preheat the oven to 350 degrees. Grease a loaf pan.

Sift the dry ingredients into a bowl. Cut in the butter with 2 knives or a pastry blender. Add the milk, orange juice, and egg. Mix just enough to dampen all the ingredients. Add the rind and nuts and mix well. Pour into the greased loaf pan and leave a slight depression in the center. Let it stand for 20 minutes before baking.

Bake for 1 hour or until a toothpick inserted in the center comes out clean.

Yields 1 loaf

The Inn St. Gemme Beauvais
78 North Main Street
Ste. Genevieve, Missouri

Homemade Corn and Wheat Bread

Cornmeal

22 ounces water, slightly above room temperature

1¼ ounces yeast, room temperature

2½ cups cooked sweet corn, cut off the cob

¼ cup finely chopped green pepper

¼ cup finely chopped red pepper

¼ cup finely chopped yellow pepper

1 tablespoon finely chopped chives

1 tablespoon finely chopped onion

1 pinch coarsely ground black pepper

1 pound 6 ounces white flour, room temperature

1 pound 6 ounces whole wheat flour, room temperature

¾ ounce salt

3 ounces honey

Preheat the oven to 400 degrees. Insert a tray of ceramic bread-baking tiles. Sprinkle a flat baking sheet with cornmeal.

Proof the yeast in the water. Mix all the vegetables and the pepper together. Let stand.

Mix the flours with the salt. Stir in the yeast mixture and add the honey. Mix well. Turn the dough out onto a lightly floured board and knead until the dough is smooth and elastic, about 10 to 12 minutes. Cover and let stand at room temperature until double in bulk. Punch down the dough, remove from the bowl, and put onto a floured surface. Cut the dough into four equal pieces and roll each piece into a rectangle 12 × 14 inches. Sprinkle with the vegetable mixture and roll into loaves, pinching the seams together. Transfer each loaf, seam side down, to the baking sheet, leaving 4 inches between the loaves. Cover with a clean cloth, put in a draft-free place and allow to double in bulk.

With a razor or sharp knife, slash the top of each loaf at 4-inch intervals.

Open the oven door and slide out the baker's rack with the tiles. In one motion, jerk the baking sheet so that the loaves slide onto the tiles. The loaves should be slid onto the tiles narrow ends first.

Bake for 10 to 15 minutes or until the loaves are nicely browned and sound hollow when tapped. Remove, cool, and serve with a little additional honey.

Yields 4 loaves

Foley's
211 East Ohio Street
Chicago, Illinois

Corn and Sage Bread

1 tablespoon dry yeast, or 1
   package compressed yeast
1/3 cup sugar, divided
1/4 cup warm water
1/3 cup shortening
1/2 teaspoon sage
1/4 cup onion flakes
1 tablespoon salt
1 cup evaporated milk plus 1 cup
   water, or 2 cups milk, scalded
3 cups unbleached flour
2 eggs, well beaten
1 cup yellow cornmeal
4 to 4½ cups flour, divided

Preheat the oven to 375 degrees. Grease 2 9 × 5 × 3–inch loaf pans. Dissolve the yeast and 1 teaspoon of the sugar in the warm water in a small bowl. Let stand for 5 to 10 minutes or until mixture expands and becomes bubbly. Set aside.

Combine the shortening, remaining sugar, sage, onion flakes, and salt with the milk and water (or milk) in a large bowl. Stir until the shortening melts.

Stir in the unbleached flour. Add the eggs, cornmeal, and reserved yeast mixture. Stir in 3½ cups of the flour. Gradually stir in enough of the remaining flour to make a stiff dough. Turn out onto a lightly floured board. Knead for 10 minutes or until the dough is smooth and elastic. Dust the board and dough with more flour if necessary to prevent sticking. Shape the dough into a ball. Place in a large, well-greased bowl. Turn the dough to grease the top. Cover with a clean towel and let rise in a warm, draft-free place for 1 to 1½ hours or until double in bulk. Punch down the dough. Turn out onto a lightly floured board. Cover and let rest for 10 minutes. Knead for 1 to 2 minutes. Cut the dough in half and shape into 2 loaves. Place the dough in pans, seam side down. Cover and let rise in a warm, draft-free place for 20 minutes or until the dough has risen to the rim of the pans. Bake for 35 to 45 minutes or until the crust is brown and the top sounds hollow when rapped with a knuckle. Remove from the pans and cool on a rack.

Yields 2 loaves

Elsah's Landing Restaurant
18 La Salle Street
Elsah, Illinois

Morel and Beer Bread

1 ounce dried morels, ground in
  a coffee mill
12 ounces beer
½ cup warm water
½ ounce dry yeast
1 teaspoon sugar
2½ cups unbleached flour
1¾ cups cake flour
2 teaspoons salt
Cornmeal

Heat the beer in a small saucepan and add the ground morels. Let this mixture cool to about 90 degrees.

Proof the yeast with the warm water and sugar for about 10 minutes. In a large bowl, mix the flours together with the salt and then add the yeast and beer mixtures. Stir until well combined and smooth. The dough should be elastic and spongy and quite wet. Place the dough in a large, greased ceramic bowl, turning the dough so it is completely coated. Cover the bowl with plastic wrap and put it in a warm place until the dough has doubled in bulk, about 1 hour.

Preheat the oven to 450 degrees. Place the dough onto a heavily floured board, working enough flour into the dough so it can be handled easily and is no longer sticky. Work the dough into a ball, and place in a bowl or pan lined with a well-floured cloth. Cover with a piece of well-oiled plastic wrap and let rise in a warm place until almost double in bulk, about 30 to 40 minutes.

Sprinkle cornmeal on an oiled baking sheet and invert the dough onto the sheet. Slash the dough as desired and bake in the oven for 20 minutes. Reduce the heat to 400 degrees and bake 10 minutes longer or until the bread is brown and sounds hollow when tapped with a knuckle.

Yields 1 loaf

Tapawingo
9502 Lake Street
Ellsworth, Michigan

Swedish Rye Bread

This bread is delicious for sandwiches or toast. It's not difficult to make and the aroma when baking is heavenly. Everyone
should make bread at least once!

2 tablespoons dry yeast
¼ cup warm water
1 teaspoon sugar
1 cup evaporated milk
3 cups water
2 tablespoons shortening
1 cup sugar
1 cup molasses
1 tablespoon salt
3 cups rye flour
9 cups white flour

Dissolve the yeast in the warm water with the teaspoon of sugar. The water should be about 110 degrees.

Combine the milk and water. Scald and cool. Add the shortening, sugar, molasses, and salt, mixing well.

Beat in the rye flour, a half cup at a time. Then add the white flour gradually, mixing with a wooden spoon, until thick. Knead in the remainder of the flour until the dough is no longer sticky. Place in a well-greased bowl and turn the dough to coat it thoroughly. Cover it with a clean towel and let rise in a warm, draft-free place until double in bulk.

Punch down and divide the dough into 4 equal pieces. Roll each out into a rectangle. Roll it up to form a loaf, pinch the ends of the dough to seal, and place the loaf in a well-greased 9 × 4–inch loaf pan.

Preheat the oven to 350 degrees while the dough rises again. When the dough has doubled, place in the oven and bake for 40 to 45 minutes or until the loaves are well browned and sound hollow when rapped with a knuckle.

Yields 4 loaves

The Swedish Pantry
916 Ludington Street
Escanaba, Michigan

Rosemary Bread

When I traveled to Ohio to collect recipes, the Chadwick was a local recommendation. It fulfilled expectations, having both a ghost and this wonderful Rosemary Bread, so good I begged a loaf to take along!

4 ounces warm water, not to
  exceed 114 degrees
¼ ounce yeast
1 teaspoon sugar
2 ounces pureed onion
1 teaspoon chopped rosemary
½ ounce bacon grease
2 ounces cold milk
1 teaspoon salt
10 ounces flour
Egg
Water

In a mixing bowl with the warm water, add the yeast, sugar, onion, rosemary, and bacon grease. Let stand for 4 minutes to allow the yeast to activate.

Add the cold milk and salt and mix together. Add the flour, mix in, and then knead for 12 minutes. Let the dough rest for 15 minutes.

Divide and shape the dough into 2 8-ounce loaves and put them on a greased cookie sheet. Let rise for 45 minutes.

While the dough is rising, preheat the oven to 350 degrees. Brush the loaves with an egg wash made with an egg beaten in a little water. Bake in the oven for approximately 20 minutes or until golden brown. The bread should sound hollow when rapped with a knuckle. Serve warm.

Yields 2 loaves

The Chadwick Inn
301 River Road
Maumee, Ohio

Maple Oatmeal Bread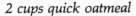

2 cups quick oatmeal
4 cups boiling water
4 tablespoons margarine
1 cup 100% Wisconsin maple
   syrup
1 tablespoon salt
2 squares block yeast or 4
   tablespoons dry yeast
2/3 cup water
6 cups flour

Soak the oatmeal in the boiling water. Dissolve the yeast in 2/3 cup water. Stir together the oatmeal, margarine, maple syrup, salt, and yeast-and-water mixture. Add 5 cups of the flour, one at a time, stirring in well. Turn out onto a floured surface, kneading and adding flour until smooth, not sticky. Place in a large oiled bowl, turning so the top of the dough is oiled. Cover and let rise in a warm, draft-free place until double in bulk, about 1 hour.

Preheat the oven to 375 degrees. Punch down the dough and divide into 4 equal parts. Pat out flat and roll into loaves. Oil the tops and place in greased loaf pans to rise. Bake for 30 minutes or until the loaves have risen and have nice, rounded tops. (The bread is done when it sounds hollow when rapped with your knuckle.)

North Star Lodge
Star Lake, Wisconsin

Potato and Caraway Bread

1 3/4 cups water
1 package compressed yeast
1 cup mashed potatoes
1 tablespoon salt
1 tablespoon caraway seeds
6 1/4 cups flour

Put the water, yeast, and mashed potatoes into a mixing bowl and mix slowly until the yeast is dissolved. Add the salt and caraway seeds. Add the flour in stages and mix well, using the dough hook on an electric mixer, if available.

Remove the dough from the mixing bowl and continue kneading it for 10 more minutes. Place the dough in a buttered bowl, turning the dough to coat it with the butter. Cover it with a clean cloth and allow it to rise in a warm, draft-free place until double in bulk.

Divide the dough in half. Flatten or roll out each half into a square approximately

12 × 12 inches. Roll up the piece from one edge as lightly as possible. Seal the seam and ends by pinching together.

Preheat the oven to 400 degrees. Place both loaves on a lightly greased cookie sheet covered with cornmeal and allow to rise until double in bulk.

When risen, paint each loaf with water and make four diagonal cuts in the top of each loaf. Place in the oven and bake for 40 minutes or until nicely browned.

Yields 2 loaves

Sarkozy's Bakery & Cafe
335 North Burdick Street
Kalamazoo, Michigan

Crusty Caraway-Rye Rolls

3 cups rye flour
2 packages dry yeast
Dash of ginger
2 tablespoons caraway seed
2¼ cups milk
¼ to ½ cup sugar
3 tablespoons shortening
1 tablespoon salt
2 eggs
4 cups white flour
Coarse salt

Combine the rye flour, yeast, ginger, and caraway seeds in a large bowl. Heat the milk, sugar, shortening, and salt until warm, approximately 120 degrees. Add to the dry ingredients. Add the eggs and beat with a wooden spoon about 3 minutes.

Stir in the white flour by hand to make a soft dough. The dough will be sticky. Place in a greased bowl, turn to grease all sides, cover, and refrigerate. Two hours before serving, shape into small balls and place on a greased cookie sheet.

Preheat the oven to 350 degrees. Let the rolls rise for 1 hour, lightly covered with a clean towel. Brush with water and sprinkle with coarse salt and caraway seeds. Bake for 20 to 25 minutes.

The Washington House Inn
W62 N573 Washington Avenue
Cedarburg, Wisconsin

Raspberry Muffins

4½ cups flour
1¼ cups sugar
2 teaspoons baking soda
½ teaspoon salt
½ teaspoon allspice
2 eggs
2 cups buttermilk
¼ pound butter, melted
2 cups fresh raspberries, washed
  and dried
Sugar (optional)

Have all the ingredients at room temperature. Preheat the oven to 425 degrees. Grease muffin tins or line with paper cups.

Sift the flour, sugar, baking soda, salt, and allspice together into a large bowl. Beat the eggs and buttermilk in another large bowl. Add the melted butter and stir to blend. Add half the dry ingredients and lightly mix. Add the remaining dry ingredients and mix lightly to moisten everything. Gently stir in the raspberries. Spoon the batter into the muffin cups, filling three-quarters full. Sprinkle with sugar, if desired.

Bake for 18 to 22 minutes or until a toothpick inserted in the center of a muffin comes out clean.

Yields 24 muffins

Quivey's Grove
6261 Nesbit Road
Madison, Wisconsin

Dutch Crust Oatmeal and Fruit Muffins

¾ cup flour
¾ cup whole wheat flour
½ cup rolled oats
½ cup packed brown sugar
2 teaspoons baking powder
1 cup cut-up or chopped fruit
2 eggs
½ cup buttermilk
½ cup melted butter

CRUST
¼ cup melted butter
¼ cup packed brown sugar
¼ cup rolled oats
¼ cup flour
1 teaspoon cinnamon

Preheat the oven to 400 degrees. Grease muffin cups or line with paper liners.

In a large bowl mix the flours, oats, sugar, and baking powder. Add the fruit and toss to coat. In a small bowl beat the eggs. Add the buttermilk and butter. Add to the flour, stirring just until mixed. Fill the muffin cups two-thirds full; top with crust mix. Bake for 15 to 25 minutes or until a toothpick inserted in the center of a muffin comes out clean.

Yields 1 dozen muffins

The Washington House Inn
W62 N573 Washington Avenue
Cedarburg, Wisconsin

Dried Cherry Scones

Michigan and Wisconsin's Door Peninsula are noted for their cherries. Dried cherries are now readily available throughout the region and by mail order. Innkeeper Gloria Krys says these are "foolproof and a wonderful addition to the breakfast table."

2 cups flour
4 teaspoons baking powder
½ teaspoon salt
¼ cup butter
3 tablespoons sugar
½ cup dried tart cherries
½ to ¾ cup milk

Preheat the oven to 450 degrees. Preheat the cookie sheet.

Sift the flour, baking powder, and salt into a bowl. Cut in the butter with a pastry blender until the mixture resembles gravel.

Add the sugar and cherries. Mix in enough milk to make a soft, but not wet, dough. On a floured surface, roll or pat out the dough to ¾ inch thick. Cut into 2-inch rounds with a cookie or biscuit cutter.

Place the rounds on the preheated cookie sheet and bake near the top of the oven for 10 to 12 minutes. These are best served fresh.

Yields a baker's dozen (13) scones

The Urban Retreat
2759 Canterbury Road
Ann Arbor, Michigan

Cranberry Muffins

Wisconsin is cranberry country and every chef or cook has a favorite recipe. These cranberry muffins are a big favorite with North Star Lodge patrons.

2 cups cranberries, crushed
½ cup sugar
2 tablespoons fresh orange juice
1 teaspoon freshly grated
   orange rind
3 eggs
¾ cup vegetable oil
1½ cups sugar
2 teaspoons vanilla extract
3 cups flour
1 teaspoon salt
1 teaspoon baking powder
1 teaspoon baking soda
1 teaspoon cinnamon
¾ cup chopped nuts (optional)

Preheat the oven to 375 degrees. Butter muffin cups or put paper liners in the cups.

Mix the cranberries with the sugar, orange juice, and rind. Mix the eggs, oil, sugar, cranberry mixture, and vanilla. Sift the dry ingredients together and add to the egg mixture. Stir in the nuts. Spoon into greased muffin tins, filling three-quarters full. Bake for 15 to 20 minutes or until a toothpick inserted in the center of one of the muffins comes out clean.

Yields 18 to 24 muffins

This recipe may also be baked as bread. Simply turn the batter into 2 8 × 4–inch greased loaf pans and bake for 50 to 60 minutes at 350 degrees.

Yields 2 loaves

North Star Lodge
Star Lake, Wisconsin

Ginger and Persimmon Muffins

There is a giant persimmon tree within steps of the kitchen door of the Southern Hotel. Innkeeper Barbara Hankins says this is both a curse and a blessing, as they are messy trees, and you have to wait for just the right combination of temperatures, especially cold ones, to make these muffins.

1¼ cups flour
¾ teaspoon baking soda
¾ teaspoon cinnamon
¾ teaspoon ground ginger
¼ teaspoon fresh grated nutmeg
¼ teaspoon ground cloves
½ cup butter, room temperature
½ cup sugar
⅓ cup light molasses
1 egg
¼ cup hot, brewed coffee
2 tablespoons sour cream
1½ teaspoons grated orange rind
½ cup fresh persimmon puree
Sugar

Preheat the oven to 375 degrees. Lightly grease 10 2½-inch muffin cups. Sift the flour, baking soda, and spices into a bowl. Using an electric mixer, cream the butter and sugar until light and fluffy. Add the molasses and egg and continue beating until smooth. Add the dry ingredients and mix well. Stir in the coffee, sour cream, and orange peel until just combined. Fold in the puree. Divide the batter into the cups. Sprinkle the tops lightly with sugar.

Bake until a cake tester or toothpick inserted in the center of one of the muffins comes out clean, about 25 to 30 minutes. Cool 5 minutes and remove from the pan.

The smell while baking is heavenly. The taste—more than a reward for the work involved.

The Southern Hotel
146 South Third Street
Ste. Genevieve, Missouri

Sweet Potato Biscuits

These are served split and piled high with thin slices of aged Missouri country ham.

2 cups flour
4 teaspoons baking powder
1 teaspoon salt
1 teaspoon nutmeg
1 teaspoon cinnamon
⅓ cup sugar
2 tablespoons butter
1 cup mashed, cooked sweet
  potatoes
½ cup heavy cream

Preheat the oven to 450 degrees. Sift the dry ingredients together. Cut in the butter until the mixture resembles coarse meal. Add the cream and the sweet potatoes, combining thoroughly. Turn out onto a lightly floured board. Knead and roll out. Cut out the biscuits, put on an ungreased baking sheet, and prick them with a fork. Bake until light brown, about 15 minutes.

America Bowman Keeping Room
Short Street at Welt
Weston, Missouri

Lucile Killeen's Potato Doughnuts

The story behind these doughnuts, in Judy Killeen-Sarkozy's words: "Lucile Killeen was my mother. Sometime in the 1940s she traveled to Chicago where she ate in a very grand hotel. She was served wonderful potato rolls. She asked for the recipe and was rebuffed.

"When she returned home to Flint, she set about re-creating the rolls. After some experimentation she came up with a recipe. These potato rolls remained a family favorite and were served at all holidays, weddings, and gatherings. It was this recipe that was adapted to make raised doughnuts, which we fried and ate on winter afternoons as an after-school treat."

⅞ cup water
½ cup plus 1 tablespoon sugar
⅞ cup mashed potatoes
2 packages compressed yeast
1 tablespoon salt
3 eggs

Place the water, sugar, mashed potatoes, yeast, and salt in a mixing bowl and blend until smooth. Add the eggs and oil and blend well. Add the flour in stages and mix the dough well, using the dough hook on an electric mixer, if available.

½ cup vegetable oil
6 cups flour
Peanut oil for frying
Cinnamon sugar or powdered
   sugar

Remove the dough from the mixer and knead well for 15 minutes on a floured board. Roll the dough into a ball and place in a well-greased bowl, turning the dough to coat the surface. Cover with a clean towel and allow it to rise in a warm place until double in bulk.

Roll out ½ inch thick and cut out pieces with a doughnut cutter. Place doughnuts on greased cookie sheets and cover lightly with a clean towel.

Put 1½ inches of peanut oil in a deep frying pan and heat to 375 degrees. Use a candy thermometer for this stage, as frying-fat at less than 375 degrees will yield greasy doughnuts and at more than 375 degrees will result in doughnuts that brown before they are done on the inside.

With a spatula, remove the risen doughnuts from the cookie sheet and lower them, one at a time, into the hot fat. Allow each one to fry about 2 minutes on a side. These doughnuts will brown quickly and will be darker than the average yeast doughnut when done. While still warm dredge them in cinnamon sugar, or wait until they are cool and dredge them in powdered sugar.

Yields approximately 12 doughnuts

Sarkozy's Bakery & Cafe
335 North Burdick
Kalamazoo, Michigan

 # APPETIZERS

An appetizer is meant to excite the eye and tease the palate into hunger. In any country, in any language, the appetizer is the prelude to a wonderful meal. It's the opening chapter, so it should be a good one—exciting enough to keep the diner eager for more.

We have become so enamored of this course that diners in a restaurant may make a meal of three or four appetizers. This is what the Spanish call *tapas*, or little plates.

Midwest chefs and cooks have caught on and the appetizers in this chapter reflect this. You will find wonderfully appetizing ideas in here for your next dinner party. Or for your family. Or just for yourself.

Asparagus Timbales with Sweet Red Pepper Sauce

SOURED CREAM
2 cups heavy cream
1 cup sour cream

TIMBALES
2 pounds asparagus, trimmed
   and washed, tips reserved
2 whole eggs, beaten
2 egg yolks
Salt
White pepper

8 ½-cup ramekins

SAUCE
1 medium sweet red pepper,
   cored, seeded, and pureed
2 ounces finely chopped shallot
¼ cup dry white wine
1 tablespoon lemon juice
¼ cup chicken stock
½ teaspoon salt
¼ teaspoon white pepper
½ cup soured cream
4 ounces unsalted butter

Red pepper, cut in diamond
   shapes, for garnish

Warm the cream and the sour cream together in a nonreactive saucepan until lightly warm to the touch (not above 110 degrees), stirring constantly. Place it in a nonreactive bowl and leave at room temperature overnight or until very thick. Cover it with plastic wrap.

Cook the reserved asparagus tips in salted water until barely cooked, 3 to 5 minutes. Drain and set aside. Preheat the oven to 325 degrees. Cook the remaining asparagus in salted water until very tender, about 20 minutes. Drain and puree in a food processor and strain through a fine mesh sieve into a bowl. Add the eggs, egg yolks, and 1¼ cups of the soured cream and season to taste with salt and pepper. Mix well. Butter the ramekins and pour in the asparagus mixture.

Place the filled ramekins in a large pan and fill the pan with water about halfway up the sides of the ramekins. Bake about 30 to 40 minutes or until a toothpick inserted in the center of one of the timbales comes out clean.

In a saucepan, combine the pureed pepper, shallots, white wine, lemon juice, stock, salt, and pepper. Reduce to ¼ cup, add ½ cup soured cream, and swirl in the butter. Season to taste.

To serve, run a knife around the edge of the timbales and invert onto a warm plate. Spoon sauce around the timbales and garnish with the reserved asparagus tips and red pepper.

Tallgrass Restaurant
1006 South State Street
Lockport, Illinois

Country Pâté

1 pound boneless pork shoulder
1 pound boneless veal shoulder
1/2 pound fresh pork fat
4 shallots, chopped
2 large garlic cloves, minced
3 bay leaves
1/4 teaspoon allspice
Salt to taste
Freshly ground black pepper to
  taste
1 rounded teaspoon thyme
1/4 cup brandy
3/4 cup white wine
3 eggs, beaten
3/4 pound good bacon
Watercress for garnish
Cornichons for garnish

Coarsely grind the pork, veal, and pork fat together. Add the chopped shallots and garlic and then the bay leaves, allspice, salt, pepper, and thyme. Add the brandy and wine. Mix well. Cover and refrigerate for 2 days, stirring once a day.

Preheat the oven to 300 degrees. Adjust the seasoning and mix in the eggs. Line a 2-quart terrine with some of the bacon and spoon the pâté mixture into the terrine, packing tightly. Cover with the remaining bacon. Bake in the preheated oven for 2 hours. Put a 4-pound weight on top and then cool the pâté in the refrigerator overnight.

Slice and serve on a platter. Garnish with fresh watercress and cornichons.

Yields 10 to 12 servings

L'Auberge
4120 Far Hills Avenue
Dayton, Ohio

Curried Duck Salad

2 roasted ducks, cooled and
  boned, the meat diced
2 large ribs celery, peeled and
  finely chopped
1 small onion, finely chopped
2 apples, diced
1/4 cup toasted sliced almonds
1 cup good mayonnaise
2/3 cup chutney, pureed
8 teaspoons good curry powder
2 1/2 teaspoons fresh lemon juice
8 teaspoons honey
1 teaspoon white vinegar
Salt and pepper

In a mixing bowl combine the mayonnaise, chutney, curry powder, lemon juice, honey, and white vinegar. Blend well. Toss with the remaining ingredients and season with salt and pepper to taste.

Chill and let marinate for at least 2 hours before serving.

Yields 8 servings as an appetizer

The Lark Restaurant
6430 Farmington Road
West Bloomfield, Michigan

Eggplant and Chèvre Sandwich with Roasted Red Pepper Sauce

1 large eggplant, 3 to 4 inches
   thick, cut in 1/3-inch slices
1/2 cup flour
4 ounces vegetable oil
8 ounces chèvre (goat cheese)
Salt and pepper to taste

SAUCE
1 medium red bell pepper
1 cup white wine
1/4 cup lime juice
1/4 cup sherry vinegar
1/4 cup chopped shallots
8 ounces unsalted butter
Salt and pepper to taste
1 tablespoon heavy cream

For the sauce, put the red pepper into a 500-degree oven and roast until the skin turns black. Remove and put into a small bowl. Cover tightly with plastic wrap and let sit for about 20 minutes. Remove the blackened skin and the core and seeds. Puree the pepper in a blender or food processor. Set aside.

While the pepper is roasting, start the sauce reduction by putting the wine, vinegar, lime juice, and shallots into a heavy, nonreactive saucepan. On high heat, let the mixture reduce until the liquid is almost gone. Remove from heat and add the cream. Cut the butter into 1-inch squares. Put the saucepan on low heat and start adding the butter, one pat at a time, until all the butter has been incorporated. Stir constantly as the butter is added. Add the red pepper puree and salt and pepper to taste. Set aside over a hot water bath to keep warm.

Lightly flour the eggplant slices. Heat a large saute pan with the vegetable oil. Put the eggplant into the pan when the oil is smoking hot. When dark brown, turn the slices over and season with salt and pepper. Put the chèvre on four of the slices, being careful not to spread the cheese all the way to the edges of the slices. When brown put the other slices on top and remove from the pan onto a paper towel. Ladle the red pepper sauce onto a plate and put the eggplant on top of the sauce.

Yields 4 servings

L'Etoile
25 North Pinckney Street
Madison, Wisconsin

Eggplant Terrine

4 medium to large eggplants,
   peeled and sliced
Kosher salt
Olive oil
1 teaspoon marjoram
1 teaspoon basil
1 teaspoon thyme
1 teaspoon oregano
12 sweet red peppers
12 sweet yellow peppers
Watercress or other fresh greens
   for garnish
Red and yellow peppers for
   garnish

Slice the eggplants approximately ⅛ inch thick. Salt the sliced eggplant with kosher salt and weigh down to press out all moisture. Leave for a half hour. Rinse, then pat dry.

Fry the eggplant in olive oil until golden brown. Drain on paper towels. Grill the peppers by impaling them on the tines of a cooking fork over a gas flame and then peel off the skin. Remove the seeds and membranes and slice.

Preheat the oven to 350 degrees. Line a terrine with parchment paper. Put down a layer of eggplant, sprinkle with the herbs, then follow with a multicolor layer of the peppers. Follow the procedure until all the eggplant and peppers are gone.

Put the terrine into a water bath or bain-marie for 45 minutes in the preheated oven. Be sure the water in the larger pan is halfway up the side of the terrine. Remove from the oven and weigh down with another terrine filled with beans or other heavy material. Cool.

When cool, slice and serve. Garnish with fresh red and yellow peppers and watercress or any fresh greens.

The 10th Street Market & Cafe
1400 West 10th Street
Cleveland, Ohio

Fettuccine con Melone

1 pound fettuccine
Salt and olive oil
1 medium cantaloupe, slightly
    overripe
4 ounces butter
Salt and pepper to taste
1½ cups heavy cream
1 cup freshly grated Parmesan
    cheese

In a large 6- to 8-quart pot, bring 3 to 4 quarts of water to a boil. Add ⅛ teaspoon salt and 1 teaspoon olive oil. Add the pasta and cook for 8 to 10 minutes or until al dente. Drain and set aside.

Peel and seed the cantaloupe. Cut into ½-inch pieces. In a large saute pan, add the butter and heat. Add the cantaloupe and saute with salt and pepper until melon is loose and soft. Let saute for 3 to 5 minutes. Add the heavy cream and bring just to a boil. Add the reserved fettuccine noodles and toss until pasta is evenly coated. Add the cheese and continue tossing. Serve hot. This dish cannot be made ahead.

Yields 4 servings

Jasper's Italian Restaurant
405 West 75th Street
Kansas City, Missouri

Sweet Potato and Ham Fritters

3 tablespoons butter
3 tablespoons flour
1 cup milk, scalded
2 eggs, separated
1 cup mashed sweet potatoes
½ cup finely chopped ham
1 tablespoon grated onion
1 teaspoon salt
½ teaspoon baking powder
¼ teaspoon pepper
¼ teaspoon nutmeg

Melt the butter in a saucepan, add the flour, and cook over a low flame for 3 to 4 minutes, stirring to blend the roux. Add the hot milk, stirring over medium heat until thickened. Remove from heat and add the egg yolks. Add the remaining ingredients, except the egg whites, and blend.

Whip the egg whites until they hold a firm shape, then fold them into the mixture.

Drop by heaping tablespoons into 375-degree oil. Cook until golden. Drain on paper towels and serve hot. This dish may be served as an appetizer or a vegetable side dish.

Public Landing Restaurant
200 West 8th Street
Lockport, Illinois

Ham and Pear Loaf

½ pound baked ham, cut into
   strips 4 inches long and ½
   inch thick
1 quart water
⅓ cup dried cherries
¾ cup ruby port
1¾ pounds ground lean pork
   shoulder
¼ pound each beef suet and
   pork fatback
½ cup heavy cream
¼ cup brandy

3 pears
2 large eggs, lightly beaten
¼ cup each dry white wine and
   apple cider
½ tablespoon each salt and
   minced garlic
1 teaspoon ground black pepper
¼ teaspoon nutmeg
½ teaspoon allspice
1⅓ tablespoons fresh chives
1½ pounds sliced bacon

Soak the ham in the water for 1 hour; soak the dried cherries in the ruby port for 1 hour. Put the pork, beef suet, fatback, and cream into a food processor and process until smooth. Transfer to a large bowl. Carefully ignite the brandy, let the flame die down, cool, and add to the meat. Refrigerate the meat mixture.

Peel, core, and cut the pears into ¼-inch cubes. Put the pears, eggs, white wine, cider, garlic, salt, pepper, nutmeg, allspice, and chives into a large bowl. Mix well and add the cherries and port. Add the pear mixture to the meat mixture.

Heat the oven to 300 degrees. Drain the ham. Line two 8 × 4–inch loaf pans with strips of bacon, letting the ends overhang the sides. Put a fourth of the meat mixture into each pan, forming an even layer. Place half the ham over each layer. Top each with the remaining meat mixture, dividing evenly. Cover the top with the remaining bacon strips and fold the overhanging bacon to cover.

Cover the pans with a double thickness of aluminum foil. Set the pans in a larger baking or roasting pan. Pour enough warm water into the larger pan to come 1½ inches up the sides of the loaf pans.

Bake for 2 hours. Remove the foil and continue baking about 30 minutes until the meat registers 160 degrees on an instant-read thermometer. Cool on a wire rack.

Cover with aluminum foil. Stack one pan on top of the other and place a can or heavy bottle on the top pan. This will help compress the loaves. Refrigerate overnight.

To unmold, dip the pans in hot water for a few seconds. Then run a knife around the edges and invert onto a plate. Cut into thin slices and serve.

Yields 2 loaves, 6 servings each

This may be refrigerated, covered, for up to 1 week.

Prairie Restaurant
500 South Dearborn
Chicago, Illinois

Smoked Trout Cheesecake

CRUST
2 cups roasted finely chopped
   hazelnuts
6 tablespoons butter

FILLING
24 ounces cream cheese, cubed
6 eggs
1 pint sour cream
⅓ cup sifted flour
Grated zest of 1 lemon
Grated zest of ½ lime
Grated zest of ½ orange
Juice of ½ lemon
1½ cups flaked smoked trout
1 cup chopped green onions
Salt and pepper to taste
Tabasco sauce to taste

Sweet and Sour Red Onions (see
   the following recipe)
Whole grain mustard
Tomatoes, diced
Cornichons

Mix 1½ cups of the nuts with the butter and use this to line the bottom of a 10-inch springform pan. Butter the sides of the pan well.

Preheat the oven to 350 degrees. Beat the cubed cream cheese until soft and creamy. Blend in the eggs one at a time until well blended. Add the sour cream, flour, zests of the lemon, lime, and orange, and lemon juice. Mix well. Stir the smoked trout and green onions into the cheese mixture and add the salt, pepper, and Tabasco.

Pour the cheese mixture into the prepared pan and bake for 1 hour. Turn off the heat and allow the cheesecake to remain in the oven for another hour. Cool to room temperature. Sprinkle the remaining nuts on top of the cake. Chill overnight. Serve with Sweet and Sour Red Onions, whole grain mustard, diced tomatoes, and cornichons.

Maldaner's
222 South Sixth Street
Springfield, Illinois

Sweet and Sour Red Onions

1 cup red wine vinegar
1 cup sugar
2 red onions, thinly sliced
2 tablespoons capers with juice

Bring the red wine vinegar to a boil in a nonreactive saucepan. Add the sugar and reduce by one quarter. Pour over the onions and then add the capers and let stand at room temperature, stirring occasionally. Serve with Smoked Trout Cheesecake.

Maldaner's
222 South Sixth Street
Springfield, Illinois

Smoked Whitefish Cheesecake

CRUST
2 tablespoons butter
¾ cup fresh bread crumbs
½ cup freshly grated Parmesan
  cheese
½ teaspoon fresh dill

FILLING
4½ tablespoons butter
2½ pounds cream cheese,
  softened
6 eggs
¾ cup grated soft white cheese
½ cup half and half
½ teaspoon salt
½ teaspoon white pepper
¾ cup chopped onion, sauteed
  until soft
¾ pound smoked whitefish,
  skinned and boned

Blend all the crust ingredients in a blender or food processor and sprinkle into a 10-inch springform pan.

Preheat the oven to 325 degrees. In a food processor, blend together the butter, cream cheese, eggs, white cheese, half and half, salt, and pepper. When thoroughly blended, add the onion and smoked whitefish.

Pour the batter into the prepared pan and wrap the bottom with aluminum foil. Place the pan into a larger pan with enough hot water to come halfway up the sides of the pan. Bake for approximately 1½ hours. Then turn off the oven and let stand for another hour. Chill well before slicing.

The Rowe Inn
County Road C48
Ellsworth, Michigan

Smoked Trout Mousse

2 8-ounce smoked rainbow trout
4 ounces cream cheese
1½ tablespoons fresh lemon juice
¼ cup chopped onion
Tabasco sauce to taste
Whole tomatoes, cut thinly into
  wheels
Lettuce and spinach leaves
  (optional)
Parsley, lemon wedges, and
  cherry tomatoes for garnish

Remove the skin and bones of 1 trout. Put the trout meat into a food processor, add the cream cheese, lemon juice, onion, and Tabasco. Process until a smooth puree has formed.

For an impressive presentation, set out the remaining whole trout on a serving tray on a bed of lettuce and spinach leaves. Place the whole tomato wheels around the fish. Put the puree on the tomato wheels and garnish with parsley, lemon wedges, and cherry tomatoes.

The Trout Haus
14536 West Freeway Drive
Forest Lake, Minnesota

Smoked Trout Puffs

PUFFS
1/2 cup water
1/2 cup milk
1/4 pound butter
1 teaspoon salt
1 1/2 teaspoons sugar
1 cup flour
5 eggs, room temperature

SMOKED TROUT SALAD
1 pound cleaned smoked trout,
    boned and skinned
5 ounces onion, finely diced
1 teaspoon Lawry seasoning salt
2 teaspoons Dijon-style mustard
1 tablespoon cream
5 ounces celery, finely diced
1 tablespoon lemon pepper
    seasoning
1 teaspoon parsley flakes
2 teaspoons ketchup
2/3 cup mayonnaise

For the puffs, heat the water, milk, butter, salt, and sugar to a boil. Add the flour all at once and with a wooden spoon over medium heat, beat and cook until it forms a large, stiff ball and is difficult to work. Remove from heat and beat in the eggs one at a time, keeping the paste stiff. Grease and flour a baking sheet. Preheat the oven to 425 degrees.

Fill a pastry bag (with a half-open tip) with the paste and pipe out little puffs about 1 inch in diameter and 1 inch high. Bake for 10 minutes without disturbing. Lower the heat to 350 degrees and bake 10 minutes more or until dry, puffed, and set.

For the salad, mix together all the ingredients. Split the puffs and fill with the trout salad. Serve.

Quivey's Grove
6261 Nesbit Road
Madison, Wisconsin

Wild Mushroom Ravioli

Wild mushrooms can be found all around Wisconsin in the spring and fall. Favorites like morels and fairy rings work very well. Even common buttons from the supermarket will work with this recipe!

RAVIOLI DOUGH
1 cup unbleached flour
1 large egg
1 large egg yolk
1/4 teaspoon salt
1 tablespoon olive oil
1 1/2 to 2 tablespoons cold water

To prepare the ravioli dough, put all the ingredients except the cold water into a food processor and process until the mixture resembles cornmeal. Add the water and process until the dough forms a ball. Wrap in plastic wrap and let rest for 1 hour at room temperature.

WILD MUSHROOM DUXELLES
3 ounces butter
⅓ cup finely chopped shallots
*1 pound wild mushrooms,
   coarsely chopped*
2 tablespoons lemon juice
3 ounces Madeira wine
½ cup heavy cream
*¼ teaspoon finely chopped
   garlic*
¼ teaspoon salt
*¼ teaspoon freshly ground
   black pepper*
*1 tablespoon chopped fresh
   tarragon*
*1 tablespoon chopped fresh
   chervil*

WILD MUSHROOM CREAM SAUCE
*½ pound wild mushrooms
   (shitake, chanterelles, black
   trumpets, etc.)*
1 cup Madeira wine
2 cups heavy cream
1 cup unsalted butter, chilled
Salt and pepper

*Fresh chervil or parsley for
   garnish*

To prepare the duxelles mixture, melt the butter in a heavy-bottomed saucepan over medium heat. Add the shallots and cook until softened. Add the mushrooms and cook until most of the moisture has evaporated, about 20 minutes. Add the Madeira and once again cook until all moisture has evaporated. Add the cream and again cook until all moisture has evaporated. Remove from heat and cool. Add the garlic, salt, pepper, tarragon, and chervil.

When the dough is rested and the duxelles is cool, assemble ravioli. Roll out the dough on a floured surface as thinly as possible. With a 3-inch cookie cutter, cut the dough into 24 rounds. In the center of 12 rounds, place about 1 tablespoon of the duxelles mixture. Moisten the edges of the dough with water and place the remaining dough rounds on top of the filled rounds. Press the edges to seal.

In a large pot, bring 2 quarts of water to a boil. Add ½ teaspoon salt and 2 ounces olive oil. Add the ravioli and poach, gently, for 5 to 8 minutes. Remove with a slotted spoon and hold in ice water.

To prepare the sauce, put the mushrooms, Madeira, and cream into a small saucepan over medium heat. Reduce to about two-thirds and slowly add the butter, a few pieces at a time, and then season with salt and pepper. Remove from heat.

Reheat the ravioli in the sauce, being careful not to heat the sauce too much. Spoon some of the sauce onto heated serving plates, add 2 to 3 ravioli, and decorate with mushrooms from the sauce and fresh chervil or parsley sprigs.

Yields 8 to 12 servings

Fleur de Lis
925 East Wells
Milwaukee, Wisconsin

SOUPS

Soup is a universal food, one that is made in almost every part of the world. It is a food that sustains working people, that refreshes and nourishes people of diverse cultures. It can be a food that entices and beguiles the appetite into wanting more. Some soups are little more than aromatic broths, an ephemeral essence, while others come perilously close to stew. All should be evocations of what the land and/or nearby bodies of water offer.

Soup vies with baking bread as to which has the more enticing aroma when cooking. To have both going at the same time is an embarrassment of riches. In these recipes when a soup calls for the use of a stock, usually beef or chicken, all our cooks would agree that making your own is best. You will be surprised at the difference it makes.

Another desirable quality of soup is its general ease of preparation. It's a forgiving food, one easily made by beginners as well as experts in the kitchen. The rewards are as ego building as they are soul satisfying. What Midwest cooks offer you here is everything from hearty Corn Chowder to elegant soup-for-breakfast Iced Strawberry Soup.

Apple Cider Soup with Cinnamon Dumplings

SOUP
½ *cup diced onion*
½ *cup diced carrot*
1 *clove garlic*
3 *apples, peeled and cored*
3 *tablespoons butter*
2 *to 3 tablespoons flour*
1 *quart apple cider*
Juice of 1 lemon
½ *teaspoon each nutmeg,*
    cinnamon, and white pepper

DUMPLINGS
2 *tablespoons butter*
2 *eggs*
6 *tablespoons flour*
1 *tablespoon minced onion*
¼ *teaspoon salt*
¼ *teaspoon cinnamon*

Cinnamon sticks

In a saucepan, saute the onions, carrots, garlic, and apples in the butter until soft. Add the flour and stir. Add the cider slowly, stirring to blend, and then cover and simmer for 20 minutes. Transfer the mixture to a food processor or blender and puree. Add the seasonings, taste, and adjust as necessary. Return to the pan and bring to a simmer.

Meanwhile, for the dumplings, beat the butter until soft. Beat the eggs and add. Stir in the rest of the ingredients. Drop the batter into the simmering liquid using a spoon. Cover the pan and simmer for about 7 minutes. Ladle into bowls and garnish with cinnamon sticks.

The Rowe Inn
County Road C48
Ellsworth, Michigan

Asparagus Vichyssoise

2 *strips bacon, chopped*
2 *ounces clarified butter*
1 *onion, chopped*
1 *rib celery, chopped*
1 *carrot, chopped*
1 *leek, cleaned and chopped*
1 *potato, peeled and chopped*
Pepper to taste
2 *ounces flour*
2 *quarts liquid (stock or water*
    plus chicken bouillon to taste)
1 *pound asparagus*
8 *ounces sour cream*
4 *ounces half and half*

Cook the bacon in the butter. Add the chopped vegetables. Let simmer for 10 minutes, stirring occasionally. Add the flour, stirring to blend evenly. Add the liquid and simmer for 45 minutes. Add the asparagus and simmer for another 7 minutes.

Puree in a food processor or blender. Add the sour cream and the half and half. Chill thoroughly.

Oakley's at the Haymarket
161 East Michigan Avenue
Kalamazoo, Michigan

Asparagus and Mushroom Soup

This rich cream soup has a marvelous fresh taste derived from its unusual combination.

4 cups chicken stock
½ pound fresh asparagus,
    washed and cut in ½-inch
    lengths
½ cup finely diced onion
6 tablespoons butter
3 tablespoons flour
½ pound fresh mushrooms,
    sliced
1 cup light cream
¼ teaspoon garlic salt
Fresh parsley

Bring the chicken stock to a simmer in a medium saucepan. Add the asparagus, cover, and cook over medium heat for 10 minutes or until asparagus is just tender.

Saute the onion in the butter in a medium saucepan over low heat for 10 minutes or until the onion is golden brown. Blend in the flour and stir over low heat for 2 to 3 minutes. Do not brown the roux.

Add the mushrooms to the onion mixture. Cover and cook over low heat for 10 minutes or until the mushrooms are tender but not limp. Stir occasionally. Gradually add the asparagus stock mixture, stirring constantly for 3 to 5 minutes until the mixture is smooth.

Add the cream and garlic salt and heat through but do not boil. Garnish with fresh parsley.

Yields 4 to 6 servings

Elsah's Landing Restaurant
18 La Salle Street
Elsah, Illinois

Beer and Cheese Soup

The America Bowman restaurant is located on the premises of the Weston Royal Brewing Company, "the oldest brewery west of the Hudson River."

½ stick butter
½ cup chopped onion
½ cup chopped celery
½ cup finely chopped carrot
½ cup chopped green onions
½ cup flour
1½ quarts hot chicken stock
1 pound shredded sharp
  cheddar cheese
1 pint warm beer
Popped popcorn

In a large saucepan, melt the butter. Saute the vegetables until they are tender, about 20 minutes. Add the flour. Stir and cook the roux until it's golden. Add the hot chicken stock, stirring until smooth. Simmer for 15 minutes. Add the cheese and warm beer. Simmer 30 minutes more. Do not allow to boil. Serve in large bowls, garnishing each serving with a handful of fresh popcorn.

America Bowman Keeping Room
Short Street at Welt
Weston, Missouri

Cauliflower and Cheddar Chowder

1 cup butter
1 cup chopped celery
1 cup chopped onions
¾ cup flour
1 quart milk
1 quart half and half
½ head cauliflower
2 cups chicken stock
2 cups diced, cooked potatoes
8 ounces grated sharp cheddar
  cheese
Salt and pepper to taste
Parsley

Melt the butter in a heavy 6-quart stock-pot. Saute the celery and onions until tender. Remove from heat and stir in the flour. Cook 1 to 2 minutes. Stir in the milk and half and half. Cook until thick. Steam the cauliflower, broken into florets, in the chicken stock. Reserve 1 cup of the liquid and add to the chowder base. Add the cauliflower, potatoes, and seasonings to the chowder base. Simmer for 10 minutes. Stir in the grated cheese. Garnish with fresh parsley.
    Yields 12 servings

Peerless Mill Inn
319 South Second Street
Miamisburg, Ohio

Corn Chowder with Fresh Herbs and Country-smoked Ham

1 tablespoon oil or bacon fat
2 baking potatoes, peeled and
   sliced
1½ cups canned corn, with juice
1 medium carrot, peeled and
   sliced
½ small onion, peeled and diced
1 quart canned chicken broth
1 cup heavy cream
1 tablespoon chicken base or 1
   bouillon cube
1 bay leaf
Thyme, tarragon, and fresh
   parsley bouquet
½ teaspoon coarsely ground
   black pepper

GARNISH
2 canned pimentos, drained and
   finely diced
1 russet potato, peeled and diced
   in ¼-inch cubes
Salt and pepper
2 tablespoons fresh herbs
   (parsley, thyme, tarragon)
¼ pound smoked ham of your
   choice, julienned

Heat the oil or bacon fat in a large pot and add the sliced potatoes, corn, carrots, and onion. Saute until slightly tender, about 5 minutes. Add the chicken stock, cream, chicken base, bay leaf, herb bouquet, and pepper. Bring to a boil and reduce to a simmer.

Simmer until the vegetables are very soft and mushy, about 1 hour. Puree in a blender or food processor on high speed until very smooth and velvety. Return the soup to the pot and add the garnishes except the ham and fresh herbs.

Cook for about a half hour more until the diced potatoes are tender. Season to taste with salt and pepper. Serve with a garnish of chopped herbs and julienned ham.

Yields 8 servings

Prairie Restaurant
500 South Dearborn
Chicago, Illinois

Fresh Corn Chowder

½ pound bacon, chopped
1 cup chopped mild yellow
  onion
4 ribs celery, chopped
½ cup flour
2 quarts chicken stock
4 small potatoes
2 teaspoons freshly cracked
  white pepper
1 teaspoon dried thyme
2 bay leaves
½ teaspoon dried marjoram
3 tablespoons chopped parsley
2 cloves garlic, minced
6 small ears sweet corn, cut off
  the cob (3 cups kernels)
2 cups light cream
Salt and pepper to taste

In a large pot, heat the bacon and saute until crisp. Remove the bacon and reserve to use as a garnish for the soup. Add the onions and celery to the bacon fat and saute until soft, being careful not to brown. Sprinkle the vegetables with the flour and continue to cook over low heat, stirring frequently, for about 10 minutes. Be careful not to brown.

Add the chicken stock and bring to a boil, stirring frequently. Meanwhile, peel and dice the potatoes. Reduce the heat to medium and add the potatoes and herbs to the simmering soup. Add the corn and simmer until the potatoes are tender, about 12 minutes. Add the cream, return to a simmer, and season with salt and pepper. Remove the bay leaves before serving. Garnish with the reserved crisp bacon.

The Rowe Inn
County Road C48
Ellsworth, Michigan

Cream of Pumpkin Soup

4 ounces butter
½ cup chopped onions
¼ cup chopped celery
2 cups canned pumpkin
2½ cups chicken stock
2 cups milk
⅛ teaspoon ground cloves
½ teaspoon sugar
1 teaspoon lemon juice
2 drops Tabasco sauce
½ teaspoon salt
¼ cup heavy cream
Croutons

Saute the onions and celery in butter for 2 to 3 minutes. Add all the remaining ingredients except the cream. Bring to a boil and reduce heat to very low, stirring occasionally for 15 minutes. Strain the soup through a fine sieve and stir in the cream. Heat again without bringing the soup to a boil. Serve very hot with croutons.

Yields 6 servings

Public Landing Restaurant
200 West 8th Street
Lockport, Illinois

Fennel Cream Soup
with Garlic Compound Butter

½ medium onion, diced
4 slices bacon, diced
2 tablespoons butter
¼ cup diced carrot
2 pounds fennel bulb, medium
    diced
12 whole black peppercorns
3 bay leaves
1½ quarts rich chicken stock
1 pint heavy cream
Kosher salt
1 stick unsalted butter, at room
    temperature
1 clove garlic, minced
3 tablespoons fresh parsley
Spinach leaves (optional)

Saute the onion and bacon in the butter over moderate heat. Add the carrots and fennel and continue cooking until the onions are transparent and the carrots slightly soft. Add the bay leaves and peppercorns and cook another 3 minutes.

Add the chicken stock and reduce about half the liquid. Add the cream and reduce slightly. While the mixture is still warm, place it in a blender or food processor and puree until smooth. Strain with a fine mesh strainer into a large saucepan. Season with salt and a little white pepper. To finish, make the garlic compound butter.

Place the unsalted butter in a mixing bowl and whip with an electric mixer until light and fluffy. Add the garlic and parsley.

Ladle the hot soup into individual soup bowls and spoon a little compound butter on top.

Note: For a more vibrant green color in the soup, the chef suggests adding a few raw spinach leaves to the soup mixture as you puree it. Add until you get the shade of green that you like. This will not affect the flavor significantly.

The 510
510 Groveland Avenue
Minneapolis, Minnesota

Norwegian Fruit Soup

According to innkeeper Mary Martin, this recipe began as a traditional Norwegian recipe and developed as guests made suggestions, like the addition of raspberries at the end. The dried sour cherries were contributed by some Michigan guests and the innkeeper now sends away to get the cherries. They were such a great addition! Maybe the recipe should be Norwegian-Canterbury Fruit Soup.

2 cups pitted prunes
1½ cups dried apricots
1 cup golden raisins
1 cup currants
1 cup dried tart cherries
1 lemon, sliced very thin
4 sticks cinnamon
½ cup pearl tapioca, soaked ½ hour
1 cup fresh or frozen raspberries

Soak the first 5 ingredients in water to cover overnight. Add the lemon and cinnamon and simmer gently, adding the tapioca after 30 minutes. Remove from heat when the fruits are tender, about 45 minutes. Add the raspberries. Serve hot or cold.

This will keep refrigerated for several weeks, if necessary.

The Canterbury Inn
723 Second Street, S.W.
Rochester, Minnesota

Potato and Celeriac Soup

1 pound peeled potatoes
2 celery root bulbs
1 cup diced onion
1 tablespoon minced garlic
Butter and olive oil
1 quart chicken stock
½ cup white wine
3 pints half and half
Salt and pepper
Chopped chives for garnish

Peel and dice the potatoes and celery root. In a heavy-bottomed pan, saute the potatoes, celery root, onion, and garlic in several tablespoons of butter and olive oil. Deglaze the pan with the white wine and add the chicken stock. Cook the mixture until the potatoes and celery root are soft. Puree in a food processor or blender.

Add the half and half and reheat, being careful not to boil. Add salt and pepper to taste and serve, garnished with the chopped chives.

Yields 8 servings

L'Etoile
25 North Pinckney Street
Madison, Wisconsin

Rutabaga Soup

4 large rutabagas
6 medium yams
1 butternut squash
3 leeks, cleaned and chopped
2 to 3 tablespoons butter
2½ cups white wine
2 tablespoons brown sugar
1 tablespoon grated fresh ginger
Salt and pepper to taste
1 cup sauteed mushrooms, drained
1 pound broccoli, thinly sliced
1 gallon homemade chicken stock
1 quart heavy cream (optional)

Peel, clean, and thinly slice the rutabagas, yams, and butternut squash. Set aside. Saute the leeks in butter. Add the white wine, brown sugar, ginger, salt, and pepper. Reduce by one-third. Add the stock and the remaining ingredients, including the prepared vegetables. Bring to a full boil. (The pot will be quite full with solids until boiling pulls water out of the vegetables.) Stir occasionally. Cook until all vegetables are tender.

Remove from heat and let cool. Puree in a food processor or blender. Reheat, stirring occasionally. Add 1 quart of heavy cream to thicken, if desired. Add salt and pepper to taste.

The Checkerberry Inn
62644 County Road 37
Goshen, Indiana

Cold Minted Split Pea Soup

2 cups dry green split peas
3 to 4 tablespoons butter
2 cups chopped onion
1 cup chopped celery
1 cup chopped carrots
2 quarts homemade chicken stock
⅛ teaspoon ground cloves
1 bay leaf
1 cup chopped fresh mint
2 ham hocks
1 teaspoon salt
White pepper to taste
1 cup heavy cream (cold)
Fresh mint sprigs for garnish

Wash the split peas thoroughly, discarding any discolored ones. In a heavy soup kettle or stockpot, saute the onions, celery, and carrots in the butter until soft. Add the stock and bring to a boil. Slowly add the peas to the simmering stock. Add the cloves, bay leaf, mint, and ham hocks and simmer, partially covered, for 1½ hours or until the peas are very soft.

Remove the ham hocks and bay leaf and puree the soup. Strain into a bowl, season with salt and pepper, and chill. Before serving, add the cream and taste again for seasoning. Serve garnished with a sprig of mint.

Yields 6 to 8 servings

Tallgrass Restaurant
1006 South State Street
Lockport, Illinois

Snowball Soup

STOCK
5 ounces butter
6 ounces flour
1 quart chicken stock

SNOWBALLS
6 ounces ground veal
1/4 teaspoon nutmeg
1 egg white
2 ounces heavy cream
Salt and pepper to taste

2 ounces Madeira wine
1 pint heavy cream
1 teaspoon chopped pimentos
1 teaspoon chopped fresh chives
    for garnish
Salt and pepper to taste

Make a roux with the flour and butter by mixing together. In a large stockpot, bring the chicken stock to a simmer and add the roux, stirring to blend. Simmer for 30 minutes. While the soup is simmering, make the snowballs.

Puree the ground veal and nutmeg in a blender or food processor. Add the heavy cream in a slow drizzle. Add the egg white, salt, and pepper and puree until all ingredients are just mixed. Make 24 balls, each about 1/4 ounce.

In a saucepan, bring 2 quarts of lightly salted water to a boil and poach the snowballs for a few minutes.

Strain the stock, which has been simmering. Add the Madeira and the heavy cream and bring just to a boil. Add the snowballs and pimentos and serve. There should be 3 snowballs per serving. Sprinkle with the chopped chives.

Yields 8 servings

The Chadwick Inn
301 River Road
Maumee, Ohio

Sugar Snap Pea Cream Soup

½ cup chopped leeks, white part
   only
½ cup diced carrot
½ cup diced celery
½ cup diced mushrooms
3 tablespoons unsalted butter
12 whole black peppercorns
3 bay leaves
1½ quarts rich chicken stock
1 pint heavy cream
Kosher salt or regular salt
2 pounds sugar snap peas, stems
   removed
Cayenne pepper
Chervil sprigs for garnish

Saute the leeks, carrots, celery, and mushrooms in the butter until the carrots are slightly soft. Add the bay leaves and peppercorns and cook for 3 to 5 minutes. Add the chicken stock and reduce one-third. Then add the cream and reduce it slightly. As the cream-and-stock mixture reduces, bring 2 quarts of water to a rapid boil and add 1 tablespoon kosher salt or 2 tablespoons regular salt. Add the sugar snap peas to the water and blanch for 1 minute.

Remove and rinse in cold water as quickly as possible. The peas should be a bright green color. Place the stock-and-cream mixture in a blender, filling the container about halfway. Add a quarter to half of the blanched peas and puree until smooth. Strain and repeat the process until all the soup mixture and peas have been used. Reheat the strained soup mixture. DO NOT BOIL. Finish with salt and cayenne pepper to taste. Serve in individual bowls and garnish with fresh chervil sprigs.

Yields 6 servings

The 510
510 Groveland Avenue
Minneapolis, Minnesota

Iced Strawberry Soup

Strawberries are grown prolifically in Missouri. Innkeeper Barbara Hankins picks and uses fresh as long as she can, then freezes plenty for use all year long.

2 pints strawberries, fresh if possible, or frozen without syrup
1 tablespoon cornstarch
1 cup orange juice
1 cup red wine (the better the wine, the better the soup)
½ cup sugar
1 cup sour cream
Whole strawberries and mint sprigs for garnish

Clean the strawberries and remove and discard the stems. Dissolve the cornstarch in the orange juice. Put the berries and orange juice with cornstarch into the food processor or blender and puree.

In a heavy-bottomed saucepan, put the puree, wine, and sugar. Cook over medium heat until thickened. While the mixture is still warm, add the sour cream. Whisk thoroughly to incorporate. Chill overnight.

Serve in glass bowls, garnished with fresh strawberries and mint sprigs.

Yields 8 generous servings

The Southern Hotel
146 South Third Street
Ste. Genevieve, Missouri

Cream of Wild Rice Soup

½ cup raw wild rice
5 cups chicken stock
3 ribs celery, diced ¼ inch
2 large carrots, diced ¼ inch
1 large onion, diced ¼ inch
2 tablespoons butter (for
* vegetables)*
5 tablespoons butter (for roux)
4 tablespoons flour
1 cup mushrooms, sliced
½ cup sherry
1 teaspoon fresh lemon juice
2½ cups half and half
¼ teaspoon white pepper
½ teaspoon salt
2 slices very crisp bacon

Simmer the wild rice in the chicken stock until the rice is soft but not mushy. Strain the rice and set aside, reserving the stock.

Saute the carrots in the 2 tablespoons butter for 4 minutes. Drain.

In a 3-quart saucepan, make the roux using the 5 tablespoons butter and 4 tablespoons flour. Cook, stirring occasionally, for 4 to 6 minutes. Add the chicken stock, reserving ½ cup for mushrooms. Whisk to a smooth mixture and simmer for 5 minutes. If lumpy, strain.

Add the vegetables and rice. Simmer 15 minutes, stirring frequently.

Simmer the mushrooms for 5 minutes in a little of the chicken stock and add the lemon juice and sherry. Add to the soup. Reduce the half and half by half and add to the soup. Season with the salt and pepper. Before serving, crumble a half slice of bacon over each bowl.

Yields 32 ounces, approximately 4 servings

Jax Cafe
University and 20th Avenues, N.E.
Minneapolis, Minnesota

Vintner's Pot

This is a hearty soup made during the annual grape crush in Ohio for workers and their families.

1 pound bulk country pork
  sausage
1 clove garlic, chopped
1 medium onion, chopped
4 medium carrots, peeled and
  chopped
3 ribs celery, chopped
1 teaspoon crushed red pepper
1 cup chopped green cabbage
2 turnips, peeled and chopped
2 potatoes, washed and
  chopped
1 bay leaf
1 teaspoon caraway seed
Chicken stock or water to cover
Ham scraps, ground (optional)

Slowly brown the sausage in a large stockpot, using a spoon to break up the sausage as it cooks. Set aside the cooked sausage, reserving the fat in the pot.

Saute the garlic, onion, carrots, celery, and crushed red pepper in the fat. Add the cabbage, turnips, potatoes, and seasonings. Cover with the chicken stock or water and simmer slowly until all the ingredients are tender. Pay attention to the liquid, being sure that it covers the ingredients and the heat is low.

When the soup is done, return the sausage to the pot. Ground-up ham scraps may be added for additional flavor.

Arnold's Bar and Grill
210 East Eighth Street
Cincinnati, Ohio

 # MEAT AND POULTRY

This is one of the longest sections in the book because there are so many varieties of meat and of poultry and because these are commonly served as the entree—this is where most cooks and chefs choose to shine.

You will notice that there are a good number of recipes for lamb and for duck. That, I think, reflects the awakening interest in new foods here in the Midwest, foods new to the average midwesterner at least. When I first moved here thirteen years ago, not many people ate lamb, which was a shame since some of the best in the world is raised right here. Midwest farm-raised lamb is some of the best I have eaten anywhere. Now, with the increasing use of lamb in restaurants, midwesterners are beginning to understand and appreciate this food.

The same is true for duck. Indiana is leading the way in producing a superior duckling. Midwest chefs and cooks have taken to the ducks with enthusiasm and imagination. In some restaurants rare duck breast may be served as often as, and sometimes more often than, rare beef.

This section includes some classics as well, and even begins with a recipe for barbecued beef. It will not taste like that cooked slowly over open pits of hickory wood, of course, but it may serve until you can get to one of those places. This recipe comes from the Hays House, which has been serving food to travelers in Council Grove, Kansas, since 1857.

As well as lamb and duck, midwestern cooks have provided some new ways to cook chicken, beef, pork, and veal. If you can't find something you'd like to eat in this chapter, you might seriously consider a vegetarian diet.

Barbecued Beef

1 beef brisket, 5 to 10 pounds

MARINADE
1 cup liquid smoke
1 cup soy sauce
1/3 cup celery seeds
1/3 cup black pepper
1/3 cup Worcestershire sauce
1/6 cup garlic granules
1/6 cup onion salt

Mix together all the ingredients in the marinade. Place the brisket, fat side up, on a large sheet of aluminum foil in a roasting pan. Pour the marinade over the beef, fold up the foil, and seal. Let stand overnight. Do not open.

Preheat the oven to 300 degrees. Put the brisket in the oven and bake for about 5 hours until fork tender.

The Hays House
112 West Main Street
Council Grove, Kansas

Roast Beef with Wild Mushroom Sauce and Chive Cornbread Dressing

1 pound 6 ounces tenderloin of
  beef
8 ounces morel mushrooms
4 ounces wood ear mushrooms
4 ounces domestic mushrooms
1 pint rich veal stock
1 cup dry white wine
1 cup heavy cream
5 minced shallots
1 clove minced garlic
1 teaspoon fresh thyme leaves
1 ounce light olive oil
Salt and pepper to taste

DRESSING
6½ ounces yellow cornmeal
6 ounces flour
½ tablespoon baking soda
½ tablespoon baking powder
½ ounce salt
¼ cup brown sugar
2 ounces melted butter
1½ cups chopped chives
1 ear corn, kernels cut off the
  cob
2 ounces melted butter
1½ cups buttermilk
1 egg, beaten

The dressing may be prepared ahead of time. Mix all the dry ingredients together in a large bowl. Preheat the oven to 325 degrees. Grease a baking pan with a 1-inch lip.

Make a well in the center of the dry ingredients and mix in the beaten egg, butter, and buttermilk. Pour the batter into the pan and bake for about 40 to 45 minutes. Let cool.

For the roast beef, rub the beef with the garlic, thyme, olive oil, salt, and pepper. Clean and cut up the mushrooms where necessary. Preheat the oven to 375 degrees.

Heat an ovenproof pan over high heat and sear the roast on all sides. Place the roast in the oven for 15 to 20 minutes. Remove the roast from the oven, take it from the pan, and keep it warm. Saute the mushrooms in the same pan and then deglaze the pan with the white wine and veal stock. Reduce this to about half the liquid, add the cream, and again reduce by half. Slice the roast.

Crumble the cornbread dressing onto four plates and pour over the sauce. Add the sliced meat and serve.

Yields 4 servings

The Whitney
4421 Woodward Avenue
Detroit, Michigan

Sauerbraten

No cookbook about the Midwest would be complete without at least one recipe for sauerbraten.

4- to 5-pound top round roast
8 ounces cider vinegar
18 ounces water
1 lemon, cut up
1 medium onion, cut up
2 bay leaves
1½ teaspoons salt
½ teaspoon whole black
*   peppercorns*
½ teaspoon whole cloves
2 cups water
⅓ to ½ cup flour
⅓ cup sugar
2 gingersnaps, crushed
Kitchen Bouquet (optional)

Place the roast in a stainless steel or earthenware crock approximately the same size as the roast. In another stainless steel pot, combine the vinegar, water, lemon, onion, and spices and bring to a boil. Pour the hot marinade over the roast, then cool to room temperature.

Place the container in the refrigerator and let the roast marinate for 3 days. Baste the roast frequently and turn twice a day to assure proper penetration of marinade.

After 3 days remove the roast from the marinade and place it in an uncovered roasting pan. Preheat the oven to 225 degrees. Set the marinade aside. Place the roast in the oven and cook approximately 2½ to 3 hours. Remove the meat from the roaster and let stand.

Add the meat juices from the roaster to the marinade. Strain and then add 1 cup of water and bring to a boil. Add the flour to the remaining cup of water and mix well. Stir it into the marinade mixture to thicken the gravy. Bring to a boil again. Remove the gravy from the heat and add the sugar and gingersnaps. Add a little Kitchen Bouquet to deepen the color of the gravy, if desired. Slice the meat and add to the gravy before serving.

Yields 8 servings

The Ox Yoke Inn®
Amana, Iowa

Rack of Lamb with Pistachio Coating and Garlic-Honey Glaze in Black Currant Sauce

GLAZE
4 ounces peeled garlic
1/4 ounce peeled ginger root
2 ounces rice wine vinegar
2/3 ounce brown sugar
1/3 ounce honey
1/3 ounce Dijon-style mustard
Salt and pepper to taste

PISTACHIO COATING
3/4 cup toasted and ground
    pistachios
1/4 cup toasted bread crumbs
1 clove oven-roasted garlic
1 oven-roasted shallot
Salt and pepper to taste

SAUCE
4 ounces double crème de cassis
4 ounces black currants in syrup
1 cup veal glacé (stock reduced
    to syrup consistency)
2 ounces heavy cream
Salt and pepper to taste

1 3-pound rack of lamb
1/2 cup garlic-honey glaze
1 cup pistachio coating
1 cup black currant sauce
8 ounces zucchini, julienned
8 ounces summer squash,
    julienned
8 ounces carrot, julienned
8 ounces leeks, julienned
1 sprig variegated sage
3 ounces butter
Salt and pepper to taste

For the glaze, place the garlic, ginger, rice wine vinegar, and brown sugar in a stainless steel saucepan. Simmer over low heat until the garlic and ginger have lightly caramelized. Remove from heat and allow to cool. Blend in a food processor until smooth. Blend in the honey, mustard, salt, and pepper to finish.

For the pistachio coating, spread the nuts, bread, shallot, and garlic together on a saute pan and place in a 350-degree oven until golden brown. Remove from the oven and cool. In a food processor or blender, puree the shallot and garlic. Add the bread crumbs. Remove from the processor and coarsely grind the nuts. Combine the nuts, bread crumbs, salt, and pepper. Mix well.

For the sauce, flame off the crème de cassis. Add the black currants and veal glacé and reduce by half. Add the cream, salt, and pepper to finish.

Preheat the oven to 375 degrees. Clean the fat and silver skin from the lamb or have your butcher do it. Thinly glaze the top side of the racks with garlic glaze and place in the oven for 20 minutes. Saute the julienned vegetables in the butter. Remove the rack of lamb from the oven and press into the pistachio coating and allow to rest for a few minutes. Add the sage, salt, and pepper. Heat the black currant sauce. Place the julienned vegetables around the sides of a large platter. Place the sauce in the center. Cut the lamb rack along the bones into chop portions. Arrange the lamb on top of the sauce in an attractive fashion and serve.

Sammy's
1400 West 10th Street
Cleveland, Ohio

Grilled Smoked Lamb Chops with Damson Plum and Ginger Glacé

MARINADE
2 cups olive oil
3 tablespoons minced garlic
3 tablespoons minced shallots
4 tablespoons quarter-cracked
    black pepper
2 tablespoons kosher salt
2 cups cabernet sauvignon
2 sprigs fresh rosemary

PLUM SAUCE
1 cup port
2 cups cabernet sauvignon
2 tablespoons minced garlic
1/2 teaspoon chili peppers
1 tablespoon diced ginger root
2 tablespoons minced shallots
1 cup Damson plum pulp,
    pureed
1 cup sugar
1/4 cup rice vinegar
1 quart demiglacé (meat stock
    reduced to a syrup
    consistency)
Salt and pepper
1/4 pound unsalted butter

12 lamb chops
2 pounds hickory chips
Fresh plums for garnish

Combine all the ingredients for the marinade and whip to blend thoroughly. Add the lamb chops and marinate for 12 to 24 hours.

Combine the port, cabernet sauvignon, garlic, chili peppers, ginger, and shallots. Reduce by half over moderate heat.

Combine the plum pulp, sugar, and rice vinegar and puree in a blender. Add to the reduction and then reduce by another one-third of the volume.

Add the demiglacé to the reduction. Bring to a boil, reduce to a simmer, and skim any scum that forms on the top. Let simmer for approximately 30 to 40 minutes.

Strain the sauce, adjust the seasoning to your personal taste with salt and pepper, and then whip in the butter, a bit at a time. Keep covered in a warm place.

Start the grill. Have on hand 2 pounds of hickory chips soaked in water for an hour or two. Let the coals burn down until the embers glow red. Cover the coals with the hickory chips to create moderate smoke. Place the marinated lamb chops on the grill and close the lid. Smoke the chops for approximately 20 to 30 minutes.

It's important that the internal temperature of the grill does not exceed 125 degrees. This will result in overcooked lamb chops. Remove the chops from the grill and keep warm.

Arrange 3 chops on each plate, bones meeting in the middle. Lightly spoon 1 to 2 tablespoons of plum sauce over the chops, garnish with the fresh plums, and serve with your favorite vegetable or potato.

The Phoenix
30 Garfield Place
Cincinnati, Ohio

Lamb Chops Raymond

12 lamb chops

MARINADE
2 cups olive oil
½ cup rosé wine
1 tablespoon finely minced fresh
    rosemary
1 tablespoon finely minced fresh
    oregano
1 tablespoon finely minced fresh
    coriander
1 tablespoon finely minced fresh
    parsley
½ teaspoon freshly cracked
    black pepper

4 cups good fresh bread crumbs

Mix together the olive oil, wine, and herbs. Marinate the lamb chops for 3 hours in the mixture.

Preheat the oven to 350 degrees. Remove the lamb chops and set aside. Strain the solids from the marinade and add 1½ cups of the liquid to the bread crumbs, tossing lightly until all the liquid is absorbed by the crumbs. Press the breading firmly onto the chops and refrigerate for ½ to 1 hour until the breading is set. Heat ½ cup olive oil in a pan. Saute the chops until golden brown, about 2 to 3 minutes on a side for medium rare. Then bake in the oven for 5 to 8 minutes. Serve with caramelized pearl onions.

Yields 4 servings

Jax Cafe
University and 20th Avenues, N.E.
Minneapolis, Minnesota

Lamb Tarragon

SAUCE
1 tablespoon lemon juice
2 tablespoons sour cream
½ teaspoon fresh chopped
    tarragon
½ teaspoon cornstarch
1 teaspoon chopped parsley
½ garlic clove, mashed
½ teaspoon Dijon-style mustard
1 tablespoon soft butter

4 lamb chops
1 tablespoon chopped green
    onions
½ cup sliced mushrooms
Fresh mint sprigs for garnish

Put all the sauce ingredients in a bowl and stir together.

Heat a saute pan over high heat. Sear the lamb chops for 1½ minutes on each side, longer for well-done meat. Remove the chops from the saute pan. Saute the onions and mushrooms in the pan for 1 minute. Pour the sauce into the saute pan and stir for 1 minute. Spoon the sauce over the lamb chops and garnish with fresh mint leaves.

The Inn St. Gemme Beauvais
78 North Main Street
Ste. Genevieve, Missouri

Braised Lamb Shanks

4 lamb shanks, about 1 pound
  each
3 tablespoons vegetable oil
1 large onion, diced
1 cup quartered fresh
  mushrooms
¾ cup diced celery
1 turnip, peeled and diced
3 tablespoons tomato paste
Salt and pepper to taste
5 tablespoons flour
¼ teaspoon black pepper
2 cloves garlic, minced
⅛ teaspoon finely chopped
  rosemary
1 pinch thyme
1 bay leaf
½ cup Burgundy
6 cups good lamb stock or beef
  stock
Fresh parsley

Preheat the oven to 350 degrees. Season the lamb shanks with salt and pepper. Heat the oil in a heavy roaster or braiser. Brown the lamb shanks on all sides. Add the onions, mushrooms, celery, and turnips and brown them.

Add the tomato paste and mix in thoroughly with the juices. Sprinkle the flour on the meat and brown lightly. Add the black pepper, garlic, rosemary, thyme, and bay leaf. Add the Burgundy and the lamb stock. Cover the roaster and braise the lamb shanks in the oven for 1 to 1 ½ hours until done.

Skim the fat off occasionally. Taste and add salt and pepper if necessary. Arrange the lamb shanks on a platter, cover with the sauce, and sprinkle with fresh chopped parsley.

The Golden Lamb
227 South Broadway
Lebanon, Ohio

Apple-stuffed Pork Loin

I made this recipe and, not having four eggs on hand, made the stuffing without eggs. It was delicious and plenty moist, so for those with concerns about cholesterol, eliminate the eggs.

5 pound boneless pork roast
2 cups apple cider

STUFFING
5 cups good bread cubes
1 cup chopped celery
1 cup chopped onions
6 apples (Melrose if possible),
    cored and chopped
1½ cups chicken stock
Dried basil to taste
Poultry seasoning to taste
Salt and pepper to taste
4 eggs, beaten

Apple slices, spiced crabapples,
    and watercress for garnish

Preheat the oven to 350 degrees. Place the boneless pork roast in a shallow roasting pan. Pour the apple cider over the pork, cover, and bake in the preheated oven for about 2 hours until tender.

While the pork cooks, prepare the stuffing. Place the bread cubes in a large bowl and set aside. Saute the celery, onions, and apples, which you have cored and chopped, in a little butter. Pour over the bread cubes, toss lightly to mix, and then pour the chicken broth over all. Mix until well blended. Add the seasonings to suit your own taste. Add the eggs to make the stuffing moist. Place in a baking pan and heat until warmed through.

Remove the roast from the pan and keep warm. Put the pan on top of the stove, add a little flour to the pan drippings, and whisk briskly. Add chicken stock as needed.

To serve, spoon the stuffing onto the plates. Carve thin slices of the pork roast and lay them on top of the stuffing. Ladle the gravy over all and garnish with fresh apple slices, spiced crabapples, and watercress.

Yields 6 to 8 servings

The Apple Farm Restaurant
262 Pearl Road
Brunswick, Ohio

Layered Loin of Pork with Fruit

1 6- to 8-pound boneless pork
  loin, well trimmed
½ pound dry, pitted prunes
½ pound dry apricot halves
½ pound white figs
½ pound black figs
2 tablespoons ginger (more if
  you love it)
½ cup candied ginger
Soy sauce
Coarse cracked black pepper
1 can crushed pineapple
  (optional)
Sugar
Triple Sec liqueur (optional)
Grapes for garnish

Work with your butcher—you need the nicest lean muscles of the loin. This weight would be about half a loin. Ask that the tenderloin be tied in, in order to get "light" and "dark" meat. Crosscuts with the fruit stuffing are more delightful-looking servings with the three colors and textures.

Gently open the roast without disturbing the butcher's work in rolling the roast. Insert as much dried fruit as you would like, poking it into all cavities in order to produce a cooked slice that is stuffed with fruit. Poke in candied and dry ginger and pour in soy sauce last. Resettle the roast, rub with more ginger and black pepper, and cover the top with crushed pineapple, letting the juice pool in the baking pan. Take the unused dry fruits and soak in water to cover. Heat to speed the plumping process but do not boil. Add sugar to taste and Triple Sec liqueur if desired.

Bake the roast in the preheated 275-degree oven until the meat thermometer registers 175 degrees. Do *not* cook to more than 175 degrees. Overdone pork is ruined pork. Figure about a half hour per pound, but use a meat thermometer.

Let the roast stand at least 15 minutes before trying to slice. Cut ¾-inch or less crosscut slices. Serve garnished with the plumped fruit and grapes. This is a fragrant, sensuous entree. A fine accompaniment is creamed, small whole red potatoes, generously flavored with dill weed and garnished with more dill weed.

Mrs. B's Historic Lanesboro Inn
101 Parkway
Lanesboro, Minnesota

Pork Medallions in Mushroom-Beer Gravy

8 pork chops, bones removed
Flour
2 tablespoons butter
½ cup chopped green onions
2 garlic cloves, minced
1 cup sliced mushrooms
½ teaspoon thyme
1 cup beer (more if necessary to
　cover)
Salt and pepper to taste
Minced parsley for garnish

Dust the chops with the flour. Heat the butter in a large iron skillet until the butter foams. Add the chops and brown well on both sides. Remove the chops and set aside. Add the onions and garlic to the skillet and saute for 2 minutes. Add the mushrooms and thyme and saute an additional 3 minutes. Return the chops to the skillet, add the beer, and bring to a boil. Reduce the heat, cover, and simmer for 1 hour. Transfer the chops to a serving platter and keep warm. Skim the fat from the sauce. Season the sauce with salt and pepper. Spoon over the chops and sprinkle with the minced parsley.

Yields 4 servings

The Palmer House
500 Sinclair Lewis Avenue
Sauk Centre, Minnesota

Pork Tenderloin with Roasted Shallots and Strawberry-Vinegar Sauce

1½ pounds trimmed pork
  tenderloin
Olive oil
8 ounces whole shallots, roasted
  and peeled
3 ounces strawberry liqueur
2 ounces strawberry vinegar
1 cup veal demiglacé (stock
  reduced to syrup consistency)
¼ cup unsalted butter
½ cup sliced fresh strawberries
3 tablespoons chopped chives
Salt and pepper to taste
Fresh strawberries for garnish

Preheat the oven to 400 degrees. In a heavy saute pan, heat the olive oil over high heat. Sear the pork tenderloin on all sides. Finish roasting in the hot oven for about 20 minutes, depending on the thickness of the tenderloin. Remove the meat from the pan and set aside. Keep warm.

Put the pan back on the stove over medium heat. Add the shallots. Add the strawberry liqueur and flame. When the flame goes out, add the vinegar. Reduce by half. Add the veal stock and stir in the butter, a little at a time. Add the strawberries, chives, salt, and pepper. Slice the pork and divide onto four plates. Pour the sauce over and garnish the plate with fresh strawberries and whatever greens you have on hand.

Yields 4 servings

L'Etoile
25 North Pinckney Street
Madison, Wisconsin

Roast Pork
with Black Currant Sauce

SAUCE
1 cup minced shallots
3 cups good currant jelly
1/4 cup black currant vinegar
3 1/2 cups beef stock
2 1/2 cups chicken stock
1 cup water
1 cup crème de cassis
1/4 teaspoon red food coloring

Pork roast, any size

Combine all the sauce ingredients in a large, heavy-bottomed saucepan. Bring to a boil and cook until reduced by half. The sauce may then be cooled to room temperature, put in a container, and stored in the refrigerator.

Preheat the oven to 350 degrees. Put the pork roast on a rack in a roasting pan and roast in the preheated oven, basting frequently. Cook until the desired degree of doneness is reached. The sauce will glaze the roast as it cooks.

Richard Perry Restaurant
The Hotel Majestic
1019 Pine Street
St. Louis, Missouri

Filet de Veau
au Cresson et Chèvre

SAUCE

12 ounces veal trimmings, finely
    chopped
2 tablespoons butter
1 small carrot, diced
1 small onion, diced
1 shallot, diced
1 rib celery, diced
1 garlic clove, minced
3 cups chicken stock
2 cups heavy cream
1 cup fresh cresson (watercress),
    blanched and pureed

24 ounces veal tenderloin
10 ounces mushrooms, pureed
2 shallots, chopped
6 ounces veal tips, ground
4 tablespoons butter
3 ounces chèvre (goat cheese),
    crumbled

Begin the sauce by sauteing the veal trimmings in 2 tablespoons of butter until well browned. Add all the vegetables and quickly add the stock. Simmer for 40 minutes, stirring occasionally. Strain, remove the vegetables and trimmings. Reduce to 4 tablespoons liquid.

Add the cream and bring to a boil. Just before finishing the sauce, whisk in the pureed watercress. Remove, set aside, and keep warm.

Trim the veal tenderloin and cut in 4-ounce slices. Pound the slices flat. Make a slit lengthwise in the center of each portion for the stuffing. Set aside.

Saute the pureed mushrooms with the shallots and veal tips in 2 tablespoons butter until dry. Stuff each veal portion with the veal-mushroom stuffing. Saute 6 to 8 minutes in the remaining 2 tablespoons of butter until lightly browned but still pink on the inside.

Serve with noodles, spoon the sauce over all, and sprinkle the crumbled chèvre on top.

Le Titi de Paris
1015 West Dundee Road
Arlington Heights, Illinois

Veal Scallops with Eggplant and Fresh Tomatoes

4 ¼-inch slices eggplant, skinned
3 ounces clarified margarine
3 ounces olive oil
6 2-ounce veal scallops, sliced
   ¼ inch thick
6 tablespoons flour
½ ounce diced shallots
3 ounces thinly sliced
   mushrooms
2 thin slices prosciutto
1 large tomato, peeled, seeded,
   and julienned
⅛ teaspoon fines herbes
2 ounces Madeira
5 ounces espagnole sauce (lightly
   thickened brown sauce)
2 ounces unsalted butter
Salt and pepper to taste
1 tablespoon chopped parsley for
   garnish

Salt and weigh down the slices of eggplant for 1 hour. Pat dry and flour the eggplant. Heat 1 ounce each of the clarified margarine and olive oil until a light haze forms over it. Add the dusted eggplant and brown on each side. Remove from the skillet and keep warm.

Pound the veal scallops thin. Heat the remaining margarine and olive oil in a large skillet, again until a light haze forms over it. Lightly flour the veal scallops, place in the skillet, season with salt and pepper, and lightly brown on one side. Turn them and degrease the skillet, removing the excess oil. Add the shallots, mushrooms, prosciutto, fresh tomatoes, and fines herbes and saute for 2 minutes. Add the Madeira over a high flame and deglaze. Add the espagnole sauce and the butter. Cook until the butter is incorporated into the sauce. Adjust the seasoning.

Place the warmed eggplant on each service plate and layer the veal over it. Place the remaining tomatoes and mushrooms over the veal scallops and pour the sauce over all. Garnish with the chopped parsley and serve.

Yields 2 servings

Ristorante Giovanni
25550 Chagrin Boulevard
Cleveland, Ohio

Veal Saltimbocca

1 pound veal leg slices
Salt and pepper
Whole sage leaves (fresh if
    possible)
16 thin slices prosciutto
16 slices good mozzarella
1 cup flour
¼ cup butter
¼ cup olive oil
⅛ cup white wine
½ cup veal stock
1 cup tomato sauce

Put the veal slices between sheets of waxed paper and pound them with the flat side of a meat cleaver to make them slightly thinner. Season them with salt and pepper, place 2 sage leaves on each (dried sage is a poor substitute but may be used if necessary), and add a slice of the prosciutto and a slice of the mozzarella. Fold the veal slices in half, secure with toothpicks, and dust with the flour.

Melt the butter with the olive oil in a large frying pan over fairly high heat. You may use two frying pans with slightly more butter and oil so that the veal may all be cooked at the same time. Add the slices of veal and brown quickly for about 2 minutes on each side. Reduce the heat and continue cooking for about 5 minutes until the veal is just tender. Do not overcook the veal. Transfer to a hot serving platter. Remove the toothpicks and keep warm. Deglaze the pan with the wine, add the veal stock and tomato sauce and reduce by a quarter. Pour over the veal and serve.

Yields 4 servings

Jasper's Italian Restaurant
405 West 75th Street
Kansas City, Missouri

Grilled Breast of Chicken with Fresh Basil–Tomato Sauce

4 chicken breasts, boned and
  halved
16 large fresh basil leaves
3 garlic cloves, peeled and
  slivered

MARINADE
1/2 cup white wine vinegar
5 tablespoons olive oil
1/2 teaspoon salt
1/4 teaspoon pepper
1 1/2 teaspoons minced garlic

FRESH BASIL–TOMATO SAUCE
1/4 cup chopped onion
1/4 cup chopped green pepper
1/2 teaspoon minced garlic
2 tablespoons butter
2 8-ounce cans tomato sauce
1/2 teaspoon salt
1/4 teaspoon pepper
1/2 cup chopped fresh basil leaves

For the chicken breasts, slide one-eighth of the garlic clove slivers and 2 basil leaves under the skin of each chicken breast half. Place the breasts in a nonreactive pan. Combine the marinade ingredients and pour over the chicken breasts. Marinate for 4 to 6 hours or overnight.

Remove the chicken breasts from the marinade. Grill over hot coals for 8 to 10 minutes on each side and serve with the fresh basil–tomato sauce.

For the sauce, saute the onion, green pepper, and garlic in the butter until the onion is tender. Stir in the canned tomato sauce. Add the salt and pepper. Simmer for 10 minutes. Add the chopped basil right before serving.

Yields 8 servings

The Heritage Restaurant
7664 Wooster Pike
Cincinnati, Ohio

Chicken in Cider

5 chicken breasts, split
¾ cup flour
1½ teaspoons salt
8 tablespoons butter
2 slices bacon, cut in thin strips
3 green onions, sliced
1½ cups sliced fresh mushrooms
¾ cup apple cider
1 cup heavy cream
¼ cup milk
Noodles, herbed or plain

Wash and dry the chicken breasts. Remove the skin. Combine the flour and salt. Coat the chicken on all sides. Melt the butter in a large skillet. Add the chicken and brown lightly on all sides. Remove the chicken. Add the bacon to the skillet and cook until crisp. Slice the white part of the onion and add to the skillet with the mushrooms. Cook over low heat for 5 minutes. Stir in the cider, cream, and milk. Simmer over low heat, stirring constantly for 5 minutes. Return the chicken to the pan. Cover the pan loosely. Cook over low heat for 45 minutes.

Serve on buttered noodles. Spoon sauce over both chicken and noodles.

Yields: 6 to 8 servings

America Bowman Keeping Room
Short Street at Welt
Weston, Missouri

Chicken Monterey

4 whole chicken breasts, skinned
  and boned
1 stick butter
¼ teaspoon basil
¼ teaspoon white pepper
¾ teaspoon oregano
¾ teaspoon marjoram
¾ teaspoon parsley
½ teaspoon salt
¼ pound Monterey Jack cheese,
  cut into 8 cubes
¾ cup flour
2 eggs, beaten
1½ cups bread crumbs, white
  and whole wheat
1 cup sauterne wine

Preheat the oven to 350 degrees. Pound the chicken breasts until very thin. Cut each in half to form equal-size pieces.

Whip the butter until fluffy. Add the herbs, mix well, and divide in half. Using one-half the butter mixture, place approximately 1 tablespoon of the mixture in the center of each breast half. Top with one cube of cheese. Roll up, tucking the ends in.

Roll the chicken pieces in flour, dip into the beaten eggs, and roll in the bread crumbs. Top each chicken piece with a dollop of butter. Bake in the oven for 20 minutes. Pour the wine over the the chicken and bake an additional 20 minutes. Baste occasionally.

Served with Parmesan fettuccine and lightly steamed vegetables.

Cindi's Cafe and Catering
222 South 9th Street
Mount Vernon, Illinois

Poulet Saute aux Poireaux et Crème de Basil

3 chickens, approximately 2
  pounds each
Butter
1 pound leeks, cleaned and
  julienned

SAUCE
3 tablespoons butter
2 tablespoons shallots
½ cup VSOP Cognac
1 cup dry white wine
3 cups chicken stock
2 cups heavy cream
1 tomato, chopped
10 fresh basil leaves
Salt and pepper

Preheat the oven to 400 degrees. Bone the chicken and saute in the butter. Place the chicken in the oven and bake for 15 minutes.

Remove the chicken and set aside. Saute the julienne of leeks in the pan juices and butter mixture for 5 minutes, remove, and reserve. Next saute the shallots until transparent.

Add the Cognac, flame, and reduce. Add the wine and reduce. Add the chicken stock and reduce to ¼ cup. Add the cream and boil for 2 minutes. Add the chopped tomato, basil leaves, and leeks. Season to taste with salt and pepper.

To serve, spoon the sauce over the chicken.

Yields 6 servings

Le Titi de Paris
1015 West Dundee Road
Arlington Heights, Illinois

Breast of Duck
Grilled with Sesame Seed Oil
and Sweet Potato Frites

6 12-ounce duck breasts
2 ounces sesame seed oil
1 garlic clove, peeled
1 pinch of fresh lemongrass

FRITES
3 to 4 medium sweet potatoes,
    peeled
Vegetable oil

Heat the coals in a grill to the glowing ember stage. Trim the fat from the duck breasts where the fat overhangs. (If the cook leaves on too much fat, the breast will dry out before the fat is rendered. In addition to cooking time, the rendering fat will continuously drop on the coals, causing blackening of the breasts with flare-ups.) Remove the duck breast fillet. Trim any silver skin from the meat side of the breast. Divide the breast into halves.

Rub the meat with the garlic clove. Brush lightly with the oil. Grill slowly to render the duck fat. Turn the breast after the skin side is rendered. Cook only 2 or 3 minutes more for medium rare. Sprinkle lightly with the lemongrass. Continue to grill. Let the duck rest.

After 5 minutes, slice each half into thin pieces. Arrange on a plate. Sprinkle with a little additional oil. Garnish with the sweet potato frites (fries).

For the frites, using a knife or mandolin, cut the sweet potatoes into slivers the size of shoestring potatoes but a little shorter. Heat vegetable oil to 340 degrees. Drop the frites into the oil and cook until crisp. Season if you wish.

Foley's
211 East Ohio Street
Chicago, Illinois

Braised and Sauteed Duck with White Wine and Garlic Sauce

3 5- to 5½-pound ducks,
   deboned
1½ quarts dry white wine
¾ pound shallots, chopped
4 bulbs garlic, approximately
   40 cloves
3 bay leaves
10 pieces fresh thyme, or ½
   tablespoon dried thyme
1 bunch parsley stems
12 peppercorns, crushed
6 juniper berries, crushed
Peanut oil for saute
3 ounces tomato paste
Salt and pepper

STOCK
Browned duck carcasses
2 onions, cut up
1 carrot, rough chopped
1 rib celery, rough chopped
2 quarts chicken stock

Start a day ahead of when you plan to serve the duck. Debone the ducks, keeping the leg and thigh together. Reserve the carcasses to make the stock.

Marinate the duck with ½ quart of the white wine, the shallots, 1 garlic bulb (peeled and chopped), and the bay leaves, thyme, parsley stems, peppercorns, and juniper berries for at least 8 hours, preferably overnight.

While the meat marinates, make the duck stock. Brown the carcasses in a 425-degree oven with the onions, carrot, and celery. Reduce the chicken stock to 1½ quarts. Put the browned duck carcasses with the vegetables in a large stockpot and add the chicken stock. Add water to cover and bring to a boil. Simmer until the stock is again reduced to 1½ quarts. Strain and reserve the stock.

Remove the duck from the marinade. Strain and reserve the marinade and the vegetable-herb mixture. Dry the leg and thigh portions of the ducks on paper towels. Saute in ¼ cup of the oil until brown on both sides. Remove from the pan and pour off two-thirds of the oil. Add the strained vegetables from the marinade. Saute 2 minutes. Return the legs and thighs to the pan. Add the marinade and the white wine. Bring to a boil. Add the tomato paste and the duck stock. Cover and simmer until the leg and thigh portions are tender, about 45 minutes. Peel the remaining three bulbs of garlic and blanch in boiling water for 4 minutes. Drain and saute for 3 minutes in 3 tablespoons of hot oil. Reserve.

Remove the duck from the pan and transfer to another pan. Degrease the sauce and strain over the duck. Add the garlic. Season with salt and pepper to taste.

Saute the duck breasts skin side down for about 5 minutes. Turn and finish cooking until medium rare. Serve 1 breast and 1 leg-and-thigh portion with sauce and garlic.

Yields 6 servings

Sanford
1547 North Jackson Street
Milwaukee, Wisconsin

Marinated Grilled Breast of Duck

MARINADE
1 cup molasses
½ cup 100% maple syrup
1½ cups honey
2 cups brown sugar
¼ cup butter
½ cup water
¼ cup port wine

Boneless, skinless duck breasts

Put all the ingredients for the marinade in a saucepan. Cook, over medium heat, stirring until thoroughly dissolved and blended. Prepare the grill, being sure to have some hickory wood or chips.

Place the duck breasts in the marinade for 30 minutes. When the embers of the grill are red, place the duck breasts on the grill. Quickly sear the outside, keeping the inside rare. Slice and serve.

Richard Perry Restaurant
The Hotel Majestic
1019 Pine Street
St. Louis, Missouri

Grilled Duck Breast with Wild Mushrooms and Green Peppercorn Sauce

*2 whole duck breasts, removed
   from carcasses (reserve the
   carcasses)*
2 whole carrots, diced
2 ribs celery, rough cut
3 leeks, split and washed
8 juniper berries
2 garlic cloves
2 bay leaves
1 sprig fresh thyme
2 tablespoons green peppercorns
*1½ cups wild mushrooms,
   chanterelles, shitakes, etc.*
2 shallots, minced
*1 cup any red wine from
   Burgundy*
2 sticks unsalted butter, melted
4 tomatoes, chopped
2 splashes Cognac
Kosher salt
*Beet-apple puree or sliced beets
   for garnish*

Preheat the oven to 350 degrees.

Remove the skin from the breasts, being careful to avoid any tearing of the flesh. Put aside.

Roast the carcasses in the oven until nice and brown. Drain the fat while roasting. (This fat is good for sauteing meat or potatoes. It may be refrigerated for a week, sometimes longer.)

Remove the roasted duck carcasses to a very large stockpot. Saute the carrots, celery, and leeks in a little of the duck fat and then add the juniper berries and garlic. Saute a minute longer and add to the stockpot with the thyme and bay leaves. Cover with water and bring to a boil. Skim the surface and simmer for at least 2 to 3 hours, skimming occasionally. Add the tomatoes for the last hour of cooking. Strain and reduce this liquid by two-thirds. Saute half the shallots and add the reduced stock and red wine and reduce until the liquid begins to thicken slightly.

Start the charcoal grill. When the coals have become white, lightly oil the breasts with olive or vegetable oil. Season with salt and pepper. Cook with the skin side down for about 4 to 5 minutes, being careful not to overcook. The breasts should be rare to medium rare. Remove to a plate and keep warm in a lukewarm oven.

To finish the sauce, turn the heat on low and place the sauce over it, whisking in unsalted butter, a tablespoon at a time, until all but 2 ounces of the butter has been used. Add the green peppercorns and Cognac. Adjust the seasoning.

Saute the mushrooms in the remaining butter or duck fat. Thinly slice the duck breasts and place them on 4 plates. Place the mushrooms on the plates, fanning them out around the duck medallions. Pour the sauce over the top of duck breasts and mushrooms. Serve either beet-apple puree or sliced beets with a little sugar and lemon to accompany the duck breasts.

Yields 4 servings

The 510
510 Groveland Avenue
Minneapolis, Minnesota

Pan-roasted Duck Breast with Dried Cherry and Port Wine Sauce

SAUCE
5 shallots, peeled and chopped
4 tablespoons cherry preserves
2 cups ruby port
2 tablespoons red wine vinegar
2 bay leaves
1 tablespoon whole black
   peppercorns
4 sprigs fresh thyme
1 quart reduced veal stock
1 stick butter
Salt and pepper to taste

4 12-ounce baby duck breasts

SWEET POTATO STRAWS
3 medium sweet potatoes for
   straws
Vegetable oil

5 tablespoons dried cherries for
   garnish
4 tablespoons chopped chives for
   garnish

To prepare the sauce, combine the shallots, preserves, port, vinegar, bay leaves, peppercorns, and thyme. Reduce slowly over a medium flame until you have a thick, syrupy glaze.

Add the reduced veal stock and reduce by about half. Add the butter, whipping in piece by piece until well incorporated. Season to taste and do not allow the sauce to boil again. Strain through a fine mesh cap and reserve in a warm place.

To cook the duck, score the skin on the breasts in a crisscross pattern, making sure to score all the way down to the meat, but being careful not to cut into the meat.

Preheat the oven to 500 degrees. Heat a saute pan over high heat until very hot and add the breasts skin side down. As soon as the fat starts to render, drain off the excess fat immediately and reduce the heat to medium low. Return the pan to the heat and repeat this sauteing, always skin side down, for another 1 to 2 minutes until the fat begins to accumulate. Drain off the excess fat once again (if you allow the fat to accumulate in the pan, the duck skin will boil in the fat instead of getting extra crispy). Repeat this cycle of sauteing and draining another 4 to 5 times.

Next, turn the duck over and sear the meat, flesh side down, briefly (for about 30 seconds). Now turn the meat skin side down again and place on the floor of the preheated oven. Bake for 6 minutes, maybe slightly less. Remove and let the meat rest for 6 to 8 minutes before slicing.

Peel the sweet potatoes and slice them into extremely thin straws. Cook the straws quickly in hot oil (about 340 degrees) and drain.

With an electric knife, slice the duck breasts into 1/4-inch slices and then split them to form oval silver-dollar-size medallions. Arrange these in a circle on a plate. Gently ladle the sauce around the outside of the duck. Add 5 to 6 dried cherries and the chopped chives. Put your sweet potato straws in the center. Serve immediately.

Prairie Restaurant
500 South Dearborn
Chicago, Illinois

FISH AND GAME

Some cooks may be disappointed at the lack of seafood in this section, but shrimp and lobster don't grow in the Great Lakes. The Midwest has superb fish and some of the more popular, like catfish and rainbow trout, are now being successfully aquacultured. This means that fresh, local fish is readily available almost everywhere in the Midwest, and this is good news both for cooks and for the health conscious. The recipes for fish included here are simple for the most part. The delicate flavor of most of our fish lends itself superbly to simple treatment.

Included in this section are game recipes. Most game, like the more popular varieties of fish, are now being farmed for sale to restaurants and specialty markets. Increasingly, game is becoming more and more available to the average consumer. This, too, is good news, both for good cooks and for the health conscious, since game birds and animals tend to have less fat than their domesticated relatives. Besides new tastes and textures, they also offer new items for menus, exciting ways to entertain. For those who hunt and fish, here are some new ideas for all that bounty.

Grilled Mississippi Catfish with Roasted Red Pepper Relish

RELISH
3 red bell peppers
2 shallots, peeled and diced
1 clove garlic, chopped
Butter
1 ounce port wine
1 ounce raspberry vinegar
Salt and pepper

CATFISH
2 tablespoons oil
1 teaspoon fresh lemon juice
½ teaspoon seasoning salt
4 8-ounce catfish fillets

Lime wheel or roasted garlic bud
* for garnish*

For the sauce, start a charcoal fire and let it burn down to red coals. Roast the red peppers whole on the grill, preferably with the lid on, until they are blackened and shriveled slightly. Turn them so they roast evenly on all sides.

Peel the tough, clear, outer skin of the peppers, removing all the blackened peel. Then cut in half and remove the seeds, membranes, and stem. Chop the peppers into small pieces or put into a food processor or blender for a few seconds.

Saute the shallots and chopped garlic in butter. Add the port and raspberry vinegar and reduce. Add the red peppers and simmer for 10 minutes. Season to taste with salt and pepper.

Combine the oil, fresh lemon juice, and seasoning salt and dredge the fish in the oil mixture. Grill the fish over the coals for about 3 minutes on a side. Before serving, spoon a strip of the red pepper relish over the fish. Garnish with a grilled lime wheel or roasted garlic bud.

Yields 4 servings

Eagle Ridge Inn and Resort
Highway 20 East
Galena, Illinois

Great Lakes Whitefish √
with Golden Tomato-Butter Sauce

SAUCE

1½ cups chopped golden
  tomatoes (out of season, use
  canned Italian plum tomatoes
  and red cherry tomatoes)
¼ cup white wine vinegar
¼ cup fresh lemon juice
2 tablespoons minced shallots
6 to 8 ounces chilled, unsalted
  butter, cut into ½-inch pieces
Salt and white pepper to taste
Sugar to taste

WHITEFISH

½ cup flour
Salt and pepper
6 fresh whitefish fillets, 8 to 10
  ounces each, pin bones
  removed
3 tablespoons clarified butter

Golden cherry or pear tomatoes
Snipped chives
Minced red bell pepper (optional)

For the sauce, heat the chopped tomatoes to a boil in a nonreactive saucepan. Simmer gently until reduced to ½ cup. Put the pulp through a fine sieve. Reserve.

Heat the vinegar, lemon juice, and shallots to a boil in a second nonreactive saucepan. Cook until reduced to 1½ tablespoons. Stir in the tomato puree.

Remove the saucepan from the heat and immediately beat in 6 to 8 ounces of chilled butter, piece by piece, until the sauce is smooth and creamy. Season with salt, pepper, and if desired, a pinch of sugar and lemon juice. Do not allow the sauce to boil. Keep warm until ready to serve the fish.

Spread the flour over the bottom of a soup plate. Stir in salt and pepper to taste. Coat the fish fillets lightly.

Heat the clarified butter in a frying pan until medium hot. Add 2 to 3 fillets as space allows, flesh side down. Saute for 3 to 4 minutes. Turn the fish over and cook, skin side down, until the flesh is just opaque. Repeat with remaining fish, adding a little more butter if necessary. To speed the process, cook the fillets in 2 pans at the same time.

Spoon the tomato-butter sauce onto 6 warm plates. Place a fillet on each plate. Garnish with cherry tomatoes cut in half, chives, and optional red pepper. Serve with new potatoes and small garden vegetables.

Tapawingo
9502 Lake Street
Ellsworth, Michigan

Sauteed Walleye Pike Wrapped in Napa Cabbage with Scallion-Butter Sauce

Walleye is really a member of the perch family. However, everyone refers to it as pike. When I checked with my home state department of natural resources fishery office, they confirmed this but could offer no explanation. Perch or pike, it's a delicious fish.

3 pounds walleye fillets,
   cleaned, trimmed, and cut
   into 6 7-ounce portions
Salt and pepper
Flour
Peanut oil
1 head Napa cabbage, cleaned
   and blanched
Grated fresh ginger
Toasted sesame seeds
1½ cups white wine
1 cup water
½ bunch fresh thyme
½ bunch fresh tarragon leaves
3 shallots, minced
1 cup heavy cream
Juice of 1 small lemon
¾ pound butter, chilled and cut
   into pieces
1 bunch green onions, minced
   green parts only
1 package enoki mushrooms,
   trimmed and divided into 6
   portions

Season the walleye portions with a generous amount of salt and pepper. Dust lightly with flour. Heat the peanut oil until very hot and saute the fillets quickly on both sides. Remove from the pan and set aside.

Preheat the oven to 400 degrees. Take the blanched Napa cabbage leaves and spread them on a work surface. Place the cooled walleye fillets in the Napa leaves. Sprinkle lightly with the ginger and sesame seeds. Wrap the cabbage around the walleye, completely enclosing the fish.

In a shallow nonreactive roasting pan, bring ½ cup of the wine and the water and thyme to a boil. Reduce the heat and simmer for 5 minutes. Place the cabbage-wrapped walleye in the pan. The walleye should be just covered with liquid. Place the pan in the oven and cook for 5 to 7 minutes.

For the sauce, place 1 cup of the wine and the minced shallots and tarragon in a saucepan and reduce until ¼ cup of the liquid remains. Add the heavy cream and reduce until ½ cup remains. Slowly whisk the butter into the mixture over low heat. Add the lemon juice and salt and pepper to taste. Strain the sauce and add the minced green onions.

To serve, spoon the sauce onto a heated plate. Place the walleye in the center and garnish the top with the sauteed enoki mushrooms.

Yields 6 servings

Sammy's
1400 West 10th Street
Cleveland, Ohio

Fresh Pan-fried Lake Perch

Swedish Pantry customers say this is the most delectable fish they've ever eaten. One customer from Florida stops by every time he's in Escanaba. The perch is always available on the Pantry's menu. This method will work with any mild white panfish—catfish is wonderful!

Fresh filleted lake perch,
*   washed and drained*
Flour
1 egg
½ cup milk
Vegetable or olive oil
Seasoning salt

Dip the fillets in an egg wash made from the egg and milk and then dredge lightly in flour.

Heat ¼ cup of the oil in a saute pan. Place the fish, skin side down, in the hot pan. Turn the heat to medium and cook until the skin side is light golden brown. Salt very lightly with a seasoning salt such as Lawry's. Turn and brown the other side. Perch cooks quickly and should not be overdone.

The Swedish Pantry
916 Ludington Street
Escanaba, Michigan

Lake Trout on Fennel, Apple, and Yo-choy with Sweet Garlic Sauce

Having said that most of the fish recipes are simple ones, I now introduce what may be the most complex recipe in the book. Sandy D'Amato won a gold medal with this recipe using a saltwater fish. He came home and adapted it for Great Lakes trout.

POTATO TIMBALES
8 ounces russet potatoes
1 ounce heavy cream
1 small garlic clove, minced
¼ teaspoon salt
⅛ teaspoon white pepper
1 pinch nutmeg
1 small egg yolk
1 ounce grated Jarlsberg cheese

GARLIC SAUCE
2 tablespoons olive oil
1 small garlic bulb, unpeeled
1 ounce sliced shallots
10 black peppercorns, crushed
¼ bay leaf
1 small sprig fresh thyme
¼ cup red wine vinegar
1 cup dry white wine
1 cup veal stock
½ cup chicken stock
1 teaspoon arrowroot
Few drops balsamic vinegar
Salt and white pepper to taste

FENNEL, APPLE, AND YO-CHOY
2 ounces fennel bulb, sliced ¼-inch thick
2 ounces apple, peeled, sliced ¼-inch thick
1½ ounces red onion, peeled, sliced ¼-inch thick
2 tablespoons olive oil
1 teaspoon lemon juice

For the potato timbales, preheat the oven to 400 degrees and butter 4 2-ounce timbale molds. Bake the potatoes until tender. Scoop them out of their skins into a mixer with a whip. Whip until smooth, then add the cream, which you have scalded with the minced garlic, salt, white pepper, and nutmeg. Add the egg yolks and cheese. Using a pastry bag, pipe the mixture into the timbale molds. Bake in the 400-degree oven for 15 to 20 minutes until golden brown.

For the garlic sauce, brush the garlic bulb with ½ tablespoon olive oil and bake in the 400-degree oven for 25 minutes. Remove from the oven and chop into coarse pieces.

In a saucepan saute the shallots in the remaining oil and then add the peppercorns, bay leaf, and thyme. Add the vinegar and bring to a boil. Add the white wine and garlic and reduce to a glaze. Add the veal and chicken stocks and reduce by one-third. Thicken to the desired consistency, put through a fine strainer, and finish the sauce with the balsamic vinegar, salt, and white pepper.

For the fennel and apple, brush with 1 tablespoon of the olive oil and season with salt and pepper. Char-grill until crisp tender and then dice. Mix the vegetables with the lemon juice and 1 tablespoon olive oil. Reserve.

Yo-choy, trimmed, long stems
removed, cut in chiffonade
1/2 tablespoon extra virgin olive
oil
1 large garlic clove, peeled,
poached 3 minutes
Salt and pepper to taste

MUSHROOM SAUSAGE
1 1/2 ounces sea scallops
1/2 ounce dried cepes
1/4 ounce dried morels
1/2 tablespoon chopped shallots
1 teaspoon olive oil
1 tablespoon Pedro Ximenez
sherry
1 tablespoon brandy
1/4 bay leaf
1/4 cup dry white wine
5 grinds fresh black pepper
1 pinch cayenne
1 tablespoon flat leaf parsley
1 teaspoon chopped chives
1/2 teaspoon salt
1 pinch white pepper
1 pinch nutmeg
1 teaspoon egg white
1/4 cup heavy cream
1 1-foot sausage casing, soaked
Oil to coat sausage

LAKE TROUT
8 3-ounce fillets of lake trout,
cut on bias
1 cup hot fish stock
1 cup white wine
1 tablespoon chopped shallots
Salt and pepper to taste
1 tablespoon unsalted butter
Buttered parchment paper

In a hot saute pan add the 1/2 tablespoon olive oil and saute the garlic clove until golden. Remove the garlic and add the yo-choy. Season with salt and pepper and toss for 5 seconds. Remove and cool. Add the yo-choy to the fennel mixture just before serving.

For the mushroom sausage, dry the scallops on a towel. Saute the shallots, cepes, and morels in the olive oil. Add the sherry and brandy and then flame. Add the white wine and reduce until dry. Remove the mushrooms and squeeze out the juices. Place the juices back in the saute pan and reduce to a glaze. Add to the mushrooms and cool.

In a small food processor, add the scallops, parsley, chives, salt, pepper, and nutmeg and process until smooth. Add the egg white to emulsify and refrigerate for 30 minutes. Finish by adding the heavy cream in a steady stream. Mix the mousse with the mushrooms and pipe into the sausage casings loosely. Tie off the sausage but leave room for expansion. Coat with oil and grill on a moderate charbroiler for a few minutes and finish in a 350-degree oven.

For the lake trout, butter a saute pan and sprinkle the shallots over the butter. Season the fillets of trout and place on a pan. Cover with the wine and stock and the buttered paper and bring up to a simmer. Place in a 300-degree oven for about 1 minute. Drain and place on the warm fennel relish. Garnish with the potato timbales and mushroom sausages. Place sauce around all and serve.

Yields 4 servings

Sanford
1547 North Jackson Street
Milwaukee, Wisconsin

Fillets of Trout Florentine

8 ounces fresh spinach, stemmed and trimmed (1 10-ounce bag, available at most supermarkets, yields the perfect amount of fresh spinach)

4 cups chicken stock

½ pound Monterey Jack cheese, grated

¼ cup ricotta cheese

3 whole trout, heads and tails removed, filleted

Olive oil

Waxed paper

Edible flowers or cherry tomatoes and lemon slices for garnish

Preheat the oven to 425 degrees. Oil a baking pan with a light olive oil. Wash the spinach and remove the stems and tough parts. Bring the chicken stock to a boil and, using a colander, blanch the spinach for 2 to 3 minutes. Remove and drain, reserving the chicken stock for another use.

Put the spinach into a bowl with the grated Monterey Jack and ricotta cheeses. Mix thoroughly.

Gently pound the trout fillets between 2 sheets of waxed paper to achieve a uniform thickness. Divide the spinach mixture into 6 portions, and place a portion on the wide end of each fillet. Roll up around the filling and tuck the loose end underneath when you place the fillet in the baking pan. Bake exactly 6 minutes. Serve immediately with wild rice, a brown rice pilaf, or a rice dish of your choice. Garnish with edible flowers such as nasturtium or with cherry tomatoes and lemon slices.

Yields 3 servings

Hillside Hotel
Ephraim, Wisconsin

Lake Superior Trout Meunière

8 small fresh trout or 4 pounds
   fresh fillets
2 cups milk
½ to ¾ cup flour
1 teaspoon salt
½ teaspoon coarsely ground
   pepper
½ teaspoon fresh dill
Vegetable oil
4 tablespoons butter
Lemon slices and fresh parsley
   for garnish

Clean the fish and rinse well under cold running water. Place the fish in a shallow pan, cover with the milk, and let stand for 30 to 45 minutes. Remove from the milk and drain but do not dry.

Coat one at a time in the flour seasoned with the salt, pepper, and dill, using additional flour as needed.

Pour enough vegetable oil into a deep heavy skillet to fill to ½-inch deep. Heat over a medium flame. Add the trout and cook until golden brown on the under side and then turn to brown the top side.

Transfer the fish to a serving platter. Pour the oil from the skillet and wipe it dry with paper toweling. Add the butter to the skillet and heat to sizzling. Pour the melted butter over the trout, garnish with lemon slices and fresh parsley, and serve.

Yields 8 servings

The Old Rittenhouse Inn
Bayfield, Wisconsin

Lasagna of Quail, Foie Gras, and Wild Mushrooms

4 quail, boned except for legs,
  each cut into 8 pieces
1½ pounds assorted wild
  mushrooms (shitakes,
  chanterelles—whatever's in
  season)
2 to 3 tablespoons butter
½ pound foie gras
1 pear
16 2 × 3–inch pieces spinach or
  wild mushroom lasagna (fresh
  pasta may be purchased in
  many specialty stores)
1½ teaspoon chopped chives
Hazelnut oil

SAUCE
½ cup cubed bacon
1 carrot, peeled and chopped
1 onion, peeled and chopped
1 rib celery, chopped
2 cups red wine
Remainder of pear
1½ quarts duck stock
2 sprigs fresh thyme
Salt and pepper to taste

Clean the mushrooms. Thinly slice half of them and cut the other half into bite-size pieces. Cut the foie gras into 8 1-ounce slices. Using a petit melon baller, cut out 32 bite-size pieces of pear, preferably with a little skin left on each one.

In a heavy-bottomed saucepan, brown the bacon, rendering the fat. Remove the bacon and reserve for another use. Brown the carrot, onion, and celery in the bacon fat, stirring to be sure the browning is even.

Deglaze the pan with the red wine and cook down to ½ cup of liquid. Add the remainder of the pear and the duck stock and reduce to 1 cup liquid, skimming to remove the foam as it cooks down. Add the thyme sprigs the last 10 minutes of cooking. Strain and season with salt and pepper. Reserve.

In a small quantity of hazelnut oil saute all the quail pieces over a medium-high heat until just past medium rare, about 1 to 1½ minutes a side. Remove from the pan and keep warm.

Simultaneously saute the mushrooms in butter in 2 separate pans—the sliced in one, the chopped in the other. Again, remove and keep warm. Next saute the foie gras pieces in a large, fairly hot pan, 4 pieces at a time. Drain the fat continuously so that the foie gras can attain a crispness. When all the pieces are cooked keep warm off to the side.

Finally cook the pasta sheets in boiling, salted water. Cook al dente and drain, tossing in a tablespoon of hazelnut oil.

Now for the fun! On each of 4 plates, put a little pile of sauteed bite-size mushroom pieces and on top of that a couple of pieces of the boneless quail. Then place a pasta sheet, then a piece of foie gras, then another pasta sheet. Add more mushrooms and quail, then pasta, then distribute the remaining foie gras, and then the last pieces of pasta. Sprinkle the larger mushroom pieces around the plates, along with the quail leg pieces and the little "pears." Spoon sauce over the lasagna, top with the chopped chives, and serve.

Yields 4 servings

Charlie Trotter's
816 West Armitage Street
Chicago, Illinois

Quail with Riesling

STUFFING
3 slices white bread, crusts
   removed
1/3 cup milk
3 chicken livers or livers from
   quail
1 tablespoon brandy
1 pinch allspice
Salt and pepper to taste

8 grape leaves
8 sheets barding fat
8 boned quail
2 tablespoons oil
4 tablespoons butter
1 pound Riesling or other
   seedless green grapes
2 tablespoons brandy
1/2 cup chicken or game stock

To make the stuffing, soak the bread with the milk. Puree lightly with the livers in a food processor or grind through the small blade of a food mill. Add the brandy and allspice.

Preheat the oven to 300 degrees. Stuff the quail with equal amounts of the bread stuffing. Wrap the quail first in the grape leaves, then in the barding fat. Secure with kitchen twine. Heat the oil and butter over medium-high heat. Brown the quail on all sides for 5 minutes. Roast breast side down in the oven for 10 minutes. Turn the quail breast side up and roast for 5 more minutes. Baste often.

Remove the quail from the pan. Unwrap and let rest. Discard the grape leaves and fat. Pour off the fat in the bottom of the roasting pan and bring to a high heat. Add the brandy and the game stock. Boil. Add the grapes and simmer gently for 3 minutes. Add butter if necessary. Serve with a mushroom polenta and pureed or sauteed squash.

Foley's
211 East Ohio Street
Chicago, Illinois

Stuffed Grouse or Quail
with Wild Rice and Orange Dressing

1½ cups wild rice
1 11-ounce can mandarin
   oranges
½ cup water chestnuts, chopped
½ cup cranberries, chopped
1 leaf fresh sage or ¼ teaspoon
   dried sage
1 teaspoon poultry seasoning
½ teaspoon onion powder
½ teaspoon salt
½ teaspoon seasoning salt
1 pinch freshly ground black
   pepper
¼ cup brown sugar
¼ cup butter, cut in chunks
1 cup chicken stock
6 grouse or 12 quail
2½ cups water, divided
¼ cup flour
1 can jellied cranberry sauce
1 tablespoon chicken base or 2
   bouillon cubes
Orange slices
Whole cranberries
Parsley sprigs

One day in advance, place the wild rice in a bowl, cover with water to 1 inch above the rice, and soak overnight.

Drain the wild rice. Place it in a saucepan with water to cover. Bring to a boil over medium heat, reduce the heat to low, and simmer until the rice is just tender, about 15 minutes, adding more water if it becomes dry. Drain if necessary. Reserve.

Drain the mandarin oranges, reserving the liquid. In a large saucepan, combine the wild rice, orange segments, water chestnuts, cranberries, sage, poultry seasoning, onion powder, salt, seasoning salt, pepper, brown sugar, butter, and chicken stock. Bring to a boil over medium heat, reduce the heat to low, and simmer uncovered about 10 minutes, stirring occasionally. Do not overstir or the fruit will break up. If the mixture becomes dry, add a little water.

Preheat the oven to 300 degrees. Stuff the grouse or quail loosely with the dressing mixture. Reserve and refrigerate any leftover dressing. Place the birds in a roasting pan just big enough to hold them. The birds should touch one another. Cover.

Bake for 2 hours. Increase the heat to 350 degrees. Uncover and bake 45 minutes longer, basting occasionally with pan juices, until the birds are browned.

Remove the birds from the roasting pan and keep warm. In a covered saucepan, reheat any leftover dressing on top of the stove over medium heat for 15 minutes or so, adding water if necessary so that the dressing does not dry out.

To prepare the gravy, transfer the roasting pan to the top of the stove over medium heat. If desired, skim off the fat. Add 2 cups of the water. Scrape the pan to loosen any bits of drippings. Add the reserved mandarin orange liquid and cranberry sauce. If desired, add the chicken base or bouillon cubes. Stir with a whisk until blended. In a small bowl or small container with a fitted lid, mix or shake the flour and remaining ½ cup of water to blend thoroughly. Stir into the gravy. Cook, stirring, until the gravy thickens.

Place the leftover dressing in the center of a large serving platter. Arrange the birds on the platter, pour a little gravy over the birds and the dressing. Garnish with the orange slices, whole cranberries, and parsley or other greens. Serve the remaining gravy separately.

Yields 6 servings

North Star Lodge
Star Lake, Wisconsin

Roasted Venison with Three-Mustard Sauce

SAUCE
2 cups heavy cream
¼ cup veal stock
2 tablespoons tarragon mustard
2 tablespoons Dijon-style mustard
2 tablespoons honey mustard
Salt and pepper

2½ pounds boneless venison loin
Flour
Salt and pepper to taste
¼ cup vegetable oil
1 ounce cracked pink peppercorns
1 ounce cracked green peppercorns
12 small red potatoes
Butter
8 ounces pompom mushrooms
8 ounces miatake mushrooms

For the sauce, combine all the ingredients in a heavy-bottomed saucepan and reduce to 1½ cups liquid over low heat. Be careful not to scorch. Season to taste with salt and pepper.

Season the venison with salt and pepper, dust with flour, and saute in the vegetable oil until golden brown on all sides. Combine the cracked peppercorns. Remove the meat from the skillet and roll in the peppercorns. If the meat is too rare, place it in a 350-degree oven to finish. Reserve and keep it warm. Blanch the potatoes in advance and finish on an open grill or quarter and saute in butter until golden brown. Slice and saute the mushrooms in butter until tender and season to taste. Reserve and keep them warm.

Heat the three-mustard sauce and place in the center of a heated platter. Remove the venison from the oven. Allow it to rest for a few minutes and then slice it thinly. Place the meat in the center of the platter on top of the sauce. Shingle the mushrooms around the roast venison and arrange the potatoes on top of the shingled mushrooms.

Yields 8 servings

Sammy's
1400 West 10th Street
Cleveland, Ohio

Venison Steaks with Mushrooms

4 to 8 venison steaks, depending
   on size
Salt and pepper
3 tablespoons clarifed butter
1 tablespoon chopped shallots or
   2 tablespoons chopped green
   onions
½ pound fresh mushrooms,
   sliced
⅓ cup Madeira or sherry
⅓ cup heavy cream

Preheat a large skillet or 2 medium ones. Season the steaks with salt and pepper. Pour the butter into the skillet and add the steaks immediately. Brown on one side and turn over. Cook to desired doneness, as you would cook beef. Transfer to a platter and keep warm. Add the shallots or green onions and mushrooms. Saute, stirring until the mushrooms turn gray. Add the wine and continue cooking over high heat until most of the juice has evaporated. Add the cream and cook down until it becomes a sauce.

   Yields 4 servings

The Golden Mushroom
18100 West Ten Mile Road
Southfield, Michigan

Rabbit with Mustard-Celery Sauce

2 2½-pound rabbits
Butter for saute
1 cup chicken stock
½ cup chopped carrot
½ cup chopped celery
½ cup chopped onion
2 ounces shallots
½ cup dry white wine
1 bay leaf
½ teaspoon celery seed
1 cup heavy cream
4 ounces butter
1 tablespoon whole grain
   mustard
Salt

Preheat the oven to 350 degrees. Remove the tenderloins, legs, and thighs. Brown the legs and thighs on both sides and place in a shallow roasting pan with the chicken stock and chopped vegetables. Bake for 1 to 1½ hours or until tender, basting frequently.

   Saute the shallots until soft. Add the juices from the roasting pan and the white wine, bay leaf, and celery seed. Reduce to ½ cup liquid. Add the heavy cream and reduce until the sauce coats the back of a spoon. Whisk in the butter, whole grain mustard, and salt to taste.

   Saute the tenderloins in butter for 2 to 3 minutes on each side. Serve the tenderloins, legs, and thighs with sauce on the side. Accompany with rice and fresh vegetables.

   Yields 4 servings

Public Landing Restaurant
200 West 8th Street
Lockport, Illinois

VEGETABLES

Vegetables have come a long way from the days when it was a duty, definitely not a pleasure, for most of us to eat them. With recipes like these there is no reason for children to hide their vegetables on the ledge underneath the dining room table as my three children once did. Discovery only came when we moved and the moving men took apart the table. The desiccated remains would have done an Egyptian tomb proud.

Happily, all three children are now grown and are able and willing to eat their vegetables in polite company. Part of the reason is the many imaginative ways there are now of serving vegetables. And here, as elsewhere, our midwestern chefs and cooks have been hard at work, coming up with some new ways of serving vegetables, as well as some of the better traditional ways.

Ciambotta

¼ cup olive oil
¾ pound onions, chopped in
   large pieces
¾ tablespoon minced garlic
¾ pound red and green peppers,
   cut into strips
¾ tablespoon dried basil
1 teaspoon oregano
½ teaspoon crushed red pepper
1 bay leaf
2½ pounds russet potatoes,
   scrubbed, cut into steak fries
¾ pound green beans, ends
   snapped off
¾ pound zucchini, cut into thick
   julienne strips
2 16-ounce cans tomatoes,
   crushed, with juice

In a large saute pan, saute the onions, garlic, peppers, herbs, and spices until softened. Add the potatoes, green beans, zucchini, and tomatoes. Stir to mix well. Pour into a heavy casserole dish and cover with foil. Bake at 350 degrees for 2 to 3 hours until the potatoes are tender.

Yield 8 to 10 servings

Arnold's Bar and Grill
210 East Eighth Street
Cincinnati, Ohio

Peas and Beet Greens

2 pounds shelled peas
2 cups chicken stock
¼ teaspoon mace
½ teaspoon thyme
1 bay leaf, crumbled
⅛ teaspoon freshly ground black
   pepper
⅛ teaspoon salt
¾ cup baby beet greens, rinsed
   and dried

Heat the chicken stock to boiling in a medium saucepan. Add the peas, mace, thyme, crumbled bay leaf, salt, and pepper. Cook, covered, for 1 minute. Add the beet greens, re-cover, and cook 1 to 2 minutes until the greens are slightly wilted. Remove from heat, adjust the seasonings, and serve immediately in heated bowls.

Mrs. B's Historic Lanesboro Inn
101 Parkway
Lanesboro, Minnesota

Fennel, Red Onion, Jicama, and Celery Compote

This makes a wonderful garnish or sauce for grilled or baked fish.

1 small-medium bulb fennel,
  diced
1 small red onion, diced
1 bulb jicama, peeled and diced
2 tablespoons olive oil
¾ cup balsamic vinegar
1 tablespoon garlic
Salt and pepper to taste

Combine all the ingredients except the balsamic vinegar in a nonreactive saucepan. Cook over low heat for 45 to 60 minutes or until the vegetables are soft but not overcooked. Add the balsamic vinegar and seasoning and cook for another 10 minutes.

Use this vegetable compote as garnish by making a cordon around a piece of grilled fish, or use as a sauce or relish over the fish.

Rigsby's Cuisine Volatile
692 North High Street
Columbus, Ohio

Bonaparte's Retreat Corn Soufflé

2 cups whole-kernel corn
1 cup milk
2 eggs, beaten
1 teaspoon salt
2 tablespoons butter
2 tablespoons flour
2 tablespoons sugar

Combine all the ingredients in an ovenproof dish, mixing well. Bake at 350 degrees for 30 minutes. Stir occasionally.

Bonaparte's Retreat
Bonaparte, Iowa

Pickled Red Cabbage

This is a traditional accompaniment to hearty meat dishes like rouladen and sauerbraten.

1 pound red cabbage, shredded
1 teaspoon salt
1 cup sugar
1 cup white vinegar
1 cup water

Put the shredded cabbage into a bowl and sprinkle with the salt. Let stand for 30 minutes. In a nonreactive saucepan combine the sugar, vinegar, and water and bring to a boil. Pour over the cabbage and stir well. When cool, refrigerate for at least 12 hours before serving. This will keep up to a week if refrigerated.

Yields 4 servings

The Ronneburg
Amana, Iowa

Sauerkraut Casserole

½ pound sliced bacon
2 cups chopped onion
2 32-ounce jars sauerkraut,
  drained and rinsed
2 cups chopped apples
2 cups chicken stock
⅓ cup packed brown sugar
½ teaspoon pepper
½ teaspoon thyme
1½ cups dry vermouth
Apple wedges for garnish

Preheat the oven to 325 degrees. In a large skillet over medium-high heat, cook the bacon until crisp. Drain and reserve. Saute the onion in the bacon drippings until limp. Stir in the remaining ingredients. Spoon the mixture into a 3-quart baking dish. Cover and bake until the liquid is absorbed, about 2 to 2½ hours. Top with the reserved bacon and the apple wedges.

Yields 10 to 12 servings

The Mason House Inn
Bentonsport, Iowa

Red Pepper Ratatouille ✓

½ pound eggplant
½ pound zucchini
3 fresh red peppers
2 fresh green peppers
1 pound tomatoes, peeled,
    seeded, and juiced
½ pound onions, thinly sliced
1 teaspoon salt
4 tablespoons olive oil
3 cloves garlic
Pepper to taste
3 tablespoons chopped parsley
½ cup fresh basil, chopped
Pine nuts or black olives
    (optional)

Dice all the vegetables as close to the same size as possible. In a large saute pan, heat the olive oil and garlic cloves. Add the onions and gradually add the other vegetables, a little of each, sprinkling in a little parsley and basil with each addition. Sprinkle with the salt and pepper. As the vegetables cook down, keep adding more until all the vegetables have been sauteed. Be careful not to let them scorch. Refrigerate for a day to let the flavors meld. Add the pine nuts or black olives when serving.

   Yields 8 to 10 servings

The Checkerberry Inn
62644 County Road 37
Goshen, Indiana

Gratin of Squash and Zucchini ✓

4 ounces butter
4 ounces olive oil
3 leeks, white part only, trimmed
    and cleaned
4 medium zucchini, peeled and
    grated
1 butternut squash, peeled and
    grated
Cayenne, salt, and pepper to
    taste
1 tablespoon tarragon
¾ cup freshly grated Parmesan
    cheese, divided
3 medium zucchini, cut in ¼-
    inch slices

Melt the butter and oil in a saucepan. Add the leeks and saute. Remove and reserve. Add the grated zucchini, saute, and remove. Add the butternut squash, saute, and remove. Reduce any remaining liquid in the saucepan to a syrup and pour over the sauteed vegetables. Season with salt, pepper, cayenne, and tarragon. Sprinkle with half the cheese.

Preheat the oven to 400 degrees. Butter a casserole dish and arrange the sliced zucchini alternating with the vegetable mixture. Sprinkle with the reserved Parmesan cheese and bake for 30 minutes.

The Moveable Feast
326 West Liberty Street
Ann Arbor, Michigan

Sweet and White Potatoes Dauphinoise

2 medium russet potatoes
2 medium yams or sweet
    potatoes
1 clove garlic, crushed
3 tablespoons unsalted butter
1½ cups heavy cream
½ cup fresh bread crumbs
Salt and pepper

Peel and parboil the potatoes, being careful not to overcook them. Drain them and slice thinly, using a food processor if you have one, when they are cool enough to handle.

Preheat the oven to 350 degrees. Butter a 2-quart baking dish and rub it with the crushed garlic. Layer the sliced potatoes, a layer of white and then a layer of sweet potato. Season with salt and pepper between the layers and top with the bread crumbs. Pour the heavy cream over all and bake until it is golden brown and the potatoes are tender, about 35 minutes.

Yields 8 to 10 servings

Lock 24 Restaurant
State Route 154
Elkton, Ohio

Sweet Potato and Cashew Bake

½ cup packed brown sugar
⅓ cup chopped cashews
½ teaspoon salt
¼ teaspoon ground ginger
2 pounds sweet potatoes,
    cooked, peeled, and cut
    crosswise into thick pieces
1 8-ounce can peach slices, well
    drained
3 tablespoons butter

Preheat the oven to 350 degrees. Combine the brown sugar, cashews, salt, and ginger. In a 10 × 6 × 2–inch baking dish, layer half the sweet potatoes, half the peaches, and a third of the brown sugar mixture. Repeat the layers and dot the top with butter. Bake, covered, for 30 minutes. Uncover and bake the mixture about 10 minutes longer. Spoon the rest of the brown sugar mixture over the potatoes before serving.

The Mason House Inn
Bentonsport, Iowa

Yam Puree

3 to 4 large yams
1 teaspoon grated orange zest
2 tablespoons butter
2 tablespoons fresh lemon juice
Salt and pepper
½ cup coarsely chopped walnuts

Bake the yams at 350 degrees until soft. Split lengthwise, scoop out the pulp, and discard the skins.

Place the pulp in a food processor, add the rest of the ingredients except the walnuts, and puree. Remove and stir in the walnuts. Serve warm.

Yields 6 servings

The Golden Mushroom
18100 West Ten Mile Road
Southfield, Michigan

SALADS

Probably no other course has undergone such a radical change as salad has in the last few years. Gone, forever if we're lucky, is the ubiquitous tuna or chicken salad in a hollowed tomato as luncheon mainstay. Even the tossed garden salad has a new image with edible flowers like pansies, violas, and nasturtiums, greens like mâche, arugula, and radicchio all enhancing its appearance, taste, and texture. With these changes have come aromatic vinegars for the dressing, flavored with herbs, fruits, and every member of the onion family.

Chefs and cooks have experimented successfully with meats new to salads and have made up variations on the more familiar. Salads are now served with warm meat and cool greens, with nuts, fruit, cheeses, and almost anything an imaginative cook can come up with.

Some of these salads are meant as a course in a meal. Others are a light meal and need only good bread and a good wine.

Asparagus and Dill Salad

2 pounds asparagus, cut into 1-
    to 2-inch pieces
1½ cups peeled and chopped
    cucumbers
1½ cups diced red bell pepper
1½ cups sliced fresh mushrooms
Red bell pepper pieces for
    garnish

DRESSING
1½ cups yogurt
½ cup mayonnaise
6 tablespoons minced fresh
    chives
3 tablespoons Dijon-style
    mustard
3 tablespoons fresh dill
½ teaspoon salt
½ teaspoon pepper

Steam the asparagus just until it is bright green. Cool, then add it to the other vegetables and toss lightly to mix.

Whisk together the ingredients for the dressing and add to the vegetable mixture. Mix gently to thoroughly coat the vegetables with dressing. Serve on a bed of fresh lettuce. Garnish with bits of red bell pepper.

Yields 8 cups

Seva Restaurant
314 East Liberty Street
Ann Arbor, Michigan

Autumn Salad with Goat Cheese

DRESSING
3 tablespoons aged cider vinegar
1 egg yolk
1 tablespoon Dijon-style mustard
Pepper to taste
6 ounces goat cheese, blue-veined
    chèvre preferred
⅔ cup olive oil
⅔ cup vegetable oil
Salt to taste

1 head frissée or chicory, cleaned
    and trimmed
1 head romaine, cleaned and
    trimmed
1 head escarole, cleaned and
    trimmed
1 small fennel bulb, julienned
½ small red cabbage, julienned
2 tablespoons chopped chives

In a food processor or blender, combine the vinegar, egg yolk, mustard, pepper, and half the goat cheese. Blend until smooth. With the motor running, slowly add the oils and season to taste with additional pepper and salt. Crumble the remaining goat cheese and reserve to sprinkle over the salads.

Prepare the greens, fennel, and cabbage. (The recipe may be prepared ahead to this point.)

In a bowl, combine the greens, fennel, and cabbage. Add a generous amount of dressing and toss. Arrange the portions on plates. Sprinkle with the goat cheese and chives before serving.

Yields 6 to 8 servings

Tapawingo
9502 Lake Street
Ellsworth, Michigan

Seared Midwest Beef Tenderloin and Vegetable Pasta Salad

SEASONING MIXTURE
2 tablespoons chopped fresh basil
2 tablespoons finely chopped
   fresh oregano
1 tablespoon finely chopped
   fresh tarragon
1 teaspoon white pepper
1 teaspoon finely chopped garlic
1 teaspoon finely chopped onion
3 tablespoons paprika
1 teaspoon salt
1 teaspoon cumin

Oil for saute

1 pound whole beef tenderloin
1 carrot, trimmed and peeled
1 zucchini, trimmed
1 small spaghetti squash, split
   and seeded

DRESSING
1/3 cup olive oil
2 to 3 tablespoons good vinegar
1 tablespoon seasoning mixture
Salt and pepper

Fresh spinach and leaf lettuce

Mix all the seasoning ingredients together thoroughly. Dust the beef tenderloin in the seasoning mixture. Reserve 1 tablespoon of the seasoning mixture for the dressing.

Lightly oil a saute pan and put it on high heat. Sear the tenderloin on all sides so it's crisp on the outside, rare on the inside. Set aside.

Shred the carrot and zucchini on the fine setting of a mandoline. Cover the spaghetti squash with plastic wrap and cook in a microwave for 20 minutes or until thoroughly cooked. Cool. Remove the "spaghetti" from the shell.

Make a dressing by combining the olive oil, vinegar, and 1 tablespoon of the seasoning mixture. Season to taste with salt and pepper. Toss the vegetables in 1/4 cup of the dressing. Slice the beef into medallions.

Arrange the spinach and lettuce on plates, place a bed of the vegetables in the center of each, overlap the beef on the vegetables, and drizzle with the remaining dressing.

Yields 6 servings

Tallgrass Restaurant
1006 South State Street
Lockport, Illinois

Lamb Salad with Blue Cheese

*12 ounces lamb cut for saute or
  grilling*
*4 cups salad greens—1 cup each
  radicchio, endive, curly
  endive, dandelion, frissée, or
  arugula*
*2 parboiled new potatoes (red,
  white, or purple)*
*4 tablespoons fresh croutons,
  rubbed with garlic, tossed
  lightly with olive oil, and
  gently toasted*
4 teaspoons blue cheese

VINAIGRETTE
3 tablespoons balsamic vinegar
½ cup olive oil
1 pinch salt
Grind of fresh black pepper
*1 tablespoon fresh chives, cut
  into ½-inch lengths*

Take the meat from the refrigerator and let it come to room temperature. Have the salad greens cleaned and refrigerated. Make the dressing and refrigerate.

Ten minutes before serving, heat the grill or saute pan. Season the meat with salt and pepper. Brush lightly with a little olive oil and cook to desired doneness. (The chef recommends rare.) Let the meat rest to warm. Toss most of the croutons and all the potatoes in a bowl. Add and toss the greens lightly with the dressing. Arrange them neatly in the middle of a large plate. Distribute the lamb around the plate. Sprinkle with the reserved croutons and the blue cheese.

Printer's Row
550 South Dearborn
Chicago, Illinois

Warm Salad of Chicken, Wild Rice, and Corn Relish

RELISH
1 cup corn kernels
½ cup chopped red onion
½ cup chopped ripe tomato
½ cup chopped green onions
¼ cup chopped parsley
½ cup peanut oil
¼ cup red wine vinegar
Salt and pepper to taste

1 cup wild rice
4 cups water
4 chicken breasts
Favorite lettuce(s)

Combine all the relish ingredients and let stand, refrigerated, at least 1 day.

Place the rice and water in a covered saucepan and cook over low heat until all the water is absorbed.

Saute or grill the chicken breasts. Slice into thin medallions.

Arrange the lettuce(s) on individual plates. Put rice in the center and arrange the chicken medallions on the rice. Spoon the relish over the chicken and serve immediately.

Yields 4 servings

Public Landing Restaurant
200 West 8th Street
Lockport, Illinois

Wild Rice and Duck Salad with Chutney Dressing

DRESSING

1 cup prepared chutney (Major Grey's)
1/2 cup honey
1/4 cup cider vinegar
1/2 teaspoon ginger
1/2 teaspoon white pepper
1/2 teaspoon dry mustard
1/2 teaspoon salt
1/2 teaspoon curry powder

SALAD

3 cups wild rice, cooked and chilled
2 cups cooked duck meat, diced and chilled
1 medium green pepper, julienned
1 medium red pepper, julienned
1 red onion, julienned
1/2 cup sliced water chestnuts
1/2 cup fresh pineapple, cut in chunks
1/2 cup mandarin oranges, drained and chilled, reserved
1/2 cup toasted, slivered almonds, reserved
Red cabbage (optional)

Combine the ingredients for the dressing in a blender or food processor and blend until smooth.

Combine all the ingredients for the salad except those to be reserved. Add the dressing and mix well. Add the mandarin oranges and toss lightly. Sprinkle with the toasted almonds at serving.

This salad is beautiful when presented in individual cups made of red cabbage leaves. Crusty French bread, scones, or biscuits make good accompaniments.

Yields 6 servings

Jax Cafe
University and 20th Avenues, N.E.
Minneapolis, Minnesota

Warm Duck Sausage Salad with Black Forest Mushrooms

SAUSAGE
1 4-pound duckling, boned and
  skinned
¾ pound lean pork
¾ pound veal stew meat
½ pound fatback
2 minced shallots
2 cloves garlic, minced
¾ teaspoon dried rosemary
¼ teaspoon chopped red pepper
  (hot)
1 jigger applejack brandy
¾ cup white wine
Salt and freshly ground black
  pepper to taste

STOCK
Reserved duck bones
1 medium carrot, chopped
1 medium onion, chopped
1 rib celery, chopped
1 tomato, chopped
¼ cup red wine vinegar
1 clove garlic
1 bay leaf
½ cup port wine

SALAD
2 bunches arugula
2 bunches mâche
1 small head curly endive
1 head endive, julienned
2 heads radicchio
1 head Bibb lettuce
2 bunches watercress, trimmed

To make the sausage, remove the skin from the duck, being careful not to puncture the skin except at the wing and leg openings. Set aside. Put the duck meat, pork, veal, and fatback through a grinder with medium-size holes. In a rectangular stainless steel pan, mix the meat with the shallots, garlic, rosemary, red pepper, brandy, white wine, salt, and pepper.

Preheat the oven to 350 degrees. Cut the reversed duck skin in half. Form the meat mixture into sausage-like cylinders. Wrap the duck skin around the sausages and tie securely with kitchen twine. Place the sausages in a roasting pan with a little water and roast in the oven for 1 hour 15 minutes. The sausage should not be cooked dry. Remove from the oven and set aside in a warm place.

Chop the duck bones and place in a 450-degree oven until they acquire a nice brown color. Pour off the excess fat and add the carrot, onion, celery, and tomato. Roast for another 20 minutes. Place the solid contents into a stockpot. Again pour off any excess fat in the roasting pan and deglaze with the red wine vinegar and port wine. Add this liquid to the solid ingredients in the stockpot. Add garlic and bay leaf. Add cold water until it covers all the ingredients. Bring to a boil and simmer for 3½ hours. Strain, pressing all liquid from the vegetables, and continue cooking until slightly thickened, like syrup.

Select 12 outer leaves from the radicchio and set aside. Wash the salad greens and pat dry or put into a salad spinner. Tear into nice bite-size pieces. Place in a salad bowl and toss with the vinaigrette.

VINAIGRETTE
1/3 cup extra virgin olive oil
1 tablespoon Dijon-style mustard
2 to 3 tablespoons vinegar
  (optional)

1/2 pound Black Forest or shitake
  mushrooms

Arrange the reserved radicchio leaves in a triangular pattern on each plate. Divide the mixed greens into equal portions and place on top of the radicchio base. Slice the duck sausage on the diagonal and attractively arrange 4 to 6 thin slices on top of the salad. Sprinkle the mushrooms over and put 3 tablespoons of the hot duck stock over the salad.

Yields 4 servings

Ristorante Giovanni
25550 Chagrin Boulevard
Cleveland, Ohio

Spinach Salad with Breast of Duck and Raspberry Vinaigrette

VINAIGRETTE
1 tablespoon Dijon-style mustard
1 egg yolk
1 shallot, minced
1/4 cup raspberry vinegar
3/4 cup olive oil
1/2 teaspoon salt
1/4 teaspoon pepper

SALAD
1 pound spinach, rinsed well and
  dried
1 head radicchio, torn into small
  pieces
1 duck breast, sauteed medium
  rare and julienned
1 orange, peeled, pith removed,
  and sectioned

Mix the Dijon-style mustard, egg yolk, and shallot together. Add the vinegar, stirring steadily. Add the olive oil slowly in a steady stream, while stirring briskly. Add the salt and pepper.

Toss the spinach and radicchio with enough of the vinaigrette to lightly coat the leaves. Place on chilled salad plates.

Mix the julienned duck breast with enough vinaigrette to lightly coat and place in the center of each salad. Place four orange segments on each salad and serve.

Yields 4 servings

Cafe le Chat
17001 Kercheval
Grosse Pointe, Michigan

Farm-raised Quail with Black Currants on Arugula and Baby Ruby Lettuces with Walnut Vinaigrette

VINAIGRETTE
1/4 *cup champagne vinegar*
3/4 *cup walnut oil*
1/4 *cup olive oil*
1 *garlic clove, minced*
Salt and pepper

10 to 12 *ounces arugula*
10 to 12 *ounces baby ruby
lettuce*
1 *cup walnuts, toasted and
slightly chopped*
4 *quail, boned and halved*
4 *ounces vegetable oil*
Flour
4 *tablespoons black currants*
Salt and pepper to taste
*Edible flowers and fresh fruit for
garnish*

To prepare the walnut vinaigrette, combine the vinegar and garlic in a nonreactive bowl. Drizzle the oils into the vinegar while whisking vigorously to emulsify. Salt and pepper to taste. Set aside.

Clean the lettuces. Dry and refrigerate. Toast the walnuts in a 325-degree oven for 5 to 8 minutes. Chop slightly.

Preheat the oven to 350 degrees. Heat the oil in a saute pan. Salt and pepper the quail and lightly dredge in flour. Saute the quail, skin side down, until golden brown. Turn the quail over and place in the oven for 2 to 3 minutes.

Lightly toss the lettuces with the vinaigrette, just to coat. Place on the upper two-thirds of each plate. Remove the quail from the oven and pat dry to remove any excess oil. Place the quail on the lower portion of the plate and garnish with black currants. Top the lettuces with the toasted walnuts. Garnish the plates with edible flowers and fresh fruit (apples and pears do nicely).

Yields 8 servings

The Baricelli Inn
2203 Cornell Road
Cleveland, Ohio

Warm Sweetbread Salad on Cool Greens

1 pound heart of sweetbreads
6 tablespoons chanterelles
2 tablespoons toasted almonds
1 tablespoon butter
2 shallots, chopped
5 tablespoons honey
2 tablespoons Dijon-style
   mustard
1 teaspoon lemon juice
Salt and pepper

DRESSING
1 tablespoon walnut oil
1 teaspoon lemon juice

Sorrel, radicchio, and other fresh
   greens

Clean and dry the greens. Julienne the radicchio.

Blanch the sweetbreads. Peel and let cool in the stock. Break the sweetbreads in ¾-inch pieces. In a saute pan, saute the sweetbreads, chanterelles, and almonds in the butter and shallots for 3 minutes.

To the sweetbread mixture, add the honey, mustard, and lemon juice. Season to taste with salt and pepper.

Toss the greens for the salad in a dressing made with the walnut oil and lemon juice. Arrange the sweetbreads on leaves of fresh sorrel, the julienne of radicchio, and other greens that you enjoy.

Yields 4 servings

Grenadier's
747 North Broadway
Milwaukee, Wisconsin

 # DESSERTS

What can be said about desserts that has not already been said? I think here, as in other parts of this book, there is a good blend of the traditional with the contemporary. In some cases, even a melding of one with the other with wonderful results. A good example of this is the Chèvre and Ginger Ice Cream from L'Etoile in Madison, Wisconsin.

Many of us have wonderful memories of homemade ice cream. I remember making ice cream with my grandfather on the back porch of my grandparents' home in Columbus, Ohio. I don't think I have ever tasted ice cream any better than that. Not, that is, until I made this recipe.

This is old-fashioned homemade ice cream, but it has a new excitement in taste and texture. It uses two things new to Midwest cuisine—*chèvre frais*, a fresh farmhouse goats' milk cheese now made in several midwestern states and fresh ginger root, a flavoring most of us have been introduced to by our new Southeast Asian neighbors.

There are plenty of old favorites here, like a pecan pie from Missouri, a rhubarb pie from Illinois, and an apple cider tart from Michigan, an intensified apple pie. Novelties in midwestern desserts would have to include the Cottage's Rhubarb Strudel, the Sanford's Cranberry and Almond Meringue Tart, and the Public Landing's Maple Rice Pudding. Since rhubarb grows everywhere and is prolific, the Cottage deserves credit for using it in the strudel, which is accompanied by a sauce and an ice—both made from that ubiquitous plant.

Baked Apples with Apricot-Rum-Raisin Sauce

6 very large, flavorful apples
(Prairie Spy, Cortland, or
McIntosh)

1½ cups apricot preserves, good
quality, not too sweet and not
too thick

¾ cup golden raisins, plumped
in hot water and drained

¾ cup dark rum

1 cup apple juice

Yogurt, heavy cream, or crème
fraîche

Preheat the oven to 350 degrees.

Core the apples, using a melon baller. Carefully peel the upper ⅓ of each apple, leaving a nice neat line. Mix the apricot preserves, plumped raisins, and rum. Place the cored apples in a glass baking dish and fill with the apricot preserve mixture.

Mix any remaining filling with the apple juice and pour around the apples. Cover the dish and bake until the apples are spoon-tender. Serve hot with yogurt, heavy cream, or crème fraîche for breakfast, brunch, or as a dessert for a simple supper. They are also good with a premium ice cream.

Pam Sherman's Bakery & Cafe
2914 Hennepin Avenue
Minneapolis, Minnesota

Bonaparte's Retreat Rhubarb Cake

1½ cups brown sugar

½ cup shortening

1 egg

1 teaspoon vanilla extract

1 teaspoon baking soda

1 cup buttermilk or sour milk

2 cups flour

2 cups fresh rhubarb, cut into ½-
inch pieces

½ cup sugar

1 teaspoon cinnamon

Preheat the oven to 350 degrees. Grease a 9 × 12–inch baking pan.

Cream together the brown sugar, shortening, egg, and vanilla. Add the baking soda to the flour and then mix together with the brown sugar mixture. Add the buttermilk (or sour milk) and fold in the rhubarb.

Pour the batter into the greased baking pan. Combine the sugar and cinnamon and sprinkle on top. Bake for 45 minutes or until a toothpick inserted in the center comes out clean.

Bonaparte's Retreat
Bonaparte, Iowa

Apple and Walnut Cake with Rum Sauce

1½ cups vegetable oil
3 eggs
2 cups sugar
2 cups flour
⅛ teaspoon ground cloves
1¼ teaspoons ground cinnamon
¼ teaspoon ground mace
1 teaspoon baking soda
1¼ teaspoons salt
1 cup whole wheat flour
1¼ cups chopped walnuts
3 cups chopped apples, peeled
   and cored
3 tablespoons brandy

RUM SAUCE
¼ pound butter
¾ cup brown sugar
⅓ cup white sugar
¼ cup orange juice
¼ cup heavy cream
¼ cup light rum

Preheat the oven to 325 degrees. Beat the vegetable oil and eggs until thick and creamy. Sift together the sugar, flour, cloves, cinnamon, mace, baking soda, salt, and whole wheat flour. Add gradually to the egg-and-oil mixture, mixing well. Add the chopped walnuts, chopped apples, and brandy. Stir until well mixed. Pour into a buttered 9-inch springform pan.

Bake for 1 hour and 15 minutes. Remove from oven and allow the cake to rest for 10 to 15 minutes. Then remove from the springform pan. Cut the cake and serve warm with the rum sauce.

For the rum sauce, melt the butter in a saucepan. Add both sugars and simmer until they dissolve. Add the orange juice, cream, and rum. Cook until slightly thickened and creamy.

The Grande Mere Inn
5800 Red Arrow Highway
Stevensville, Michigan

Flourless Chocolate Cake with Vanilla Sauce

Chocolate is not a midwestern ingredient in that it does not grow here. It is an American ingredient, however, since it originates in Central America and parts of the Caribbean. And as much of the population here as elsewhere is addicted to it, the book would not be complete without at least one very chocolate recipe.

10 ounces semisweet chocolate
4 ounces unsalted butter
6 eggs, separated
1 cup sugar
2 teaspoons crème de cacao
½ teaspoon vanilla extract
Cream of tartar
Salt
Butter
Flour

SAUCE
2½ cups milk
½ vanilla bean
6 egg yolks
½ cup sugar
Grated peel of ½ lemon

Preheat the oven to 375 degrees. Butter and flour an 8½-inch springform pan. Melt the chocolate with the butter in a double boiler over hot but not boiling water. Keep the melted chocolate warm.

Beat the egg yolks in a mixing bowl at high speed, gradually adding ¾ cup sugar. Beat until the yolk mixture is pale yellow in color, about 4 minutes. Add the melted chocolate mixture to the yolk mixture and beat until completely smooth. Then add in the crème de cacao, adding the vanilla at the same time. Beat the egg whites with a pinch of salt and a pinch of cream of tartar until soft peaks form. Gradually add the remaining ¼ cup of sugar into the whites. Continue beating until stiff but not dry. Fold the whites carefully into the chocolate mixture and pour the batter evenly into the springform pan.

Bake for 15 minutes at 375 degrees. Then reduce the oven temperature to 350 degrees and bake for another 15 minutes. Reduce the oven temperature to 250 degrees and bake 30 minutes longer. Turn off the oven, prop open the door, and allow the cake to remain in the oven for another 30 minutes. Remove the cake from the oven and cover with a lightly dampened towel. Let stand 10 minutes. Remove the towel and cool the cake completely. Press the top of the cake lightly to smooth the top. Remove the springform pan, inverting the cake onto a serving platter.

For the sauce, combine the milk and vanilla bean. Combine the egg yolks and sugar with a balloon whisk, slowly adding the vanilla-flavored milk and grated lemon peel.

Heat the mixture, stirring constantly, until it coats the back of a spoon lightly. Put a serving of sauce on each plate and place a piece of the cake on the sauce.

Yields 8 to 10 servings

Ristorante Giovanni
25550 Chagrin Boulevard
Cleveland, Ohio

Port St. Louis Chocolate-bottom Cheesecake

6 ounces semisweet chocolate
   morsels
½ cup sugar
1¼ cups graham cracker crumbs
2 tablespoons sugar
4 ounces butter, melted
16 ounces cream cheese, softened
¾ cup sugar
1 teaspoon vanilla extract
4 eggs
½ cup sour cream

Preheat the oven to 325 degrees. Over hot, but not boiling, water put the chocolate morsels together with the ½ cup sugar. Heat until the morsels melt and the mixture is smooth. Remove from heat and set aside.

In a small bowl, combine the graham cracker crumbs, 2 tablespoons sugar, and melted butter. Mix well and pat firmly into a 9-inch springform pan, covering the bottom and extending 1 inch up the sides. Set aside.

In a large bowl, beat the cream cheese until light and creamy. Gradually beat in ¾ cup sugar. Mix in the sour cream and vanilla and then add the eggs one at a time, beating well after each addition. Divide the batter in half. Stir the melted chocolate mixture into the first half. Pour into the crumb-lined pan. Cover with the remaining batter. Bake for 50 minutes. Cool in the open oven for 30 minutes. Refrigerate until ready to serve.

Yields a 9-inch cheesecake

Port St. Louis
15 North Central Avenue
St. Louis, Missouri

Cherry Clafoutis

1 pound cherries, pitted
½ cup kirsch
1 tablespoon sugar

PASTRY
1 cup flour
2 tablespoons sugar
¼ teaspoon salt
6 tablespoons unsalted butter
1 egg yolk
½ teaspoon vanilla extract
1 tablespoon fresh lemon juice

FILLING
4 eggs
1 cup heavy cream
½ cup sugar
1 teaspoon vanilla extract
2 tablespoons cake flour
2 tablespoons kirsch

Put the cherries into a large bowl. Add the kirsch and sugar. Let marinate for 2 hours, stirring occasionally.

For the pastry, mix the flour, sugar, and salt in a large bowl. Cut in the butter until the mixture resembles coarse crumbs. Make a well in the center of the flour mixture and add the egg yolk, vanilla, and lemon juice. Mix with a fork until the dough gathers into a ball. Wrap and refrigerate for 30 minutes.

Preheat the oven to 325 degrees. Roll out the dough on a lightly floured surface. Fit into a 10-inch tart pan with removable bottom. Refrigerate for 5 minutes.

For the filling, mix the eggs, cream, sugar, vanilla, flour, and kirsch together. Drain the cherries. Remove the pan with dough from the refrigerator. Arrange the cherries carefully in the tart pan. Carefully pour the egg-and-cream mixture over the cherries.

Bake for 40 to 45 minutes until a knife inserted 1 inch from the edge and withdrawn is clean. Do not overbake. Cool on a wire rack, serve warm.

Yields 8 servings

Le Français
269 South Milwaukee Street
Wheeling, Illinois

Prune and Armagnac Flan

15 ounces chopped prunes
8 ounces Armagnac
1½ cups sugar
1½ tablespoons water
1 cup milk
3 cups cream
6 extra large eggs
6 egg yolks
¾ cup sugar

First soak the prunes in the Armagnac for 24 hours.

Butter 12 4-ounce ramekins. In a heavy-bottomed skillet, put the 1½ cups sugar and the 1½ tablespoons water. Cook over medium heat, stirring constantly, until you have a caramel. The sugar will melt and turn a soft brown color, and the consistency will thicken. Pour the caramel into the molds, dividing evenly.

Preheat the oven to 300 degrees. Combine the milk and cream. Mix the eggs and yolks with the sugar. Stir the milk-and-cream mixture into the eggs. Squeeze the Armagnac out of the prunes and add the Armagnac to the custard mixture. Pour the custard into the molds, distributing evenly. Distribute the chopped prunes evenly into each mold.

Place the molds in a large, fairly deep baking pan. Fill with hot water halfway up the sides of the molds. Bake for 1½ hours, periodically checking the water level to be sure it remains fairly constant.

Cool. Chill. Turn out and serve.

Yields 12 servings

Charlie Trotter's
816 West Armitage Street
Chicago, Illinois

Dutch Apple Cobbler

1 pastry for 9-inch pie crust

FILLING
1 cup sugar
2 tablespoons flour
½ teaspoon cinnamon
6 cups peeled, sliced apples
¼ teaspoon nutmeg
⅛ teaspoon ginger
⅓ cup cream

TOPPING
1 cup rolled oats
⅓ cup flour
½ cup brown sugar
½ teaspoon cinnamon
¼ teaspoon salt
⅓ cup butter

Preheat the oven to 375 degrees.

Roll out the pastry to fit an 8- or 9-inch square pan. Put it in the bottom of the pan. Mix the filling ingredients together, tossing lightly to coat all the apples. Put into the unbaked crust.

Rub the topping ingredients together with fingers until a coarse meal texture is obtained. Sprinkle over filling. Bake for an hour. Serve warm with whipped cream, ice cream, or a topping of your choice.

Yields 8 to 9 servings

Stephenson's Apple Farm Restaurant
16401 East 40 Highway
Kansas City, Missouri

Pumpkin Ice Cream with Cranberry-Raspberry Sauce

ICE CREAM
½ gallon premium vanilla ice cream
1 cup canned pumpkin
2 teaspoons cinnamon
½ teaspoon ground cloves
½ teaspoon nutmeg
1 tablespoon rum extract

CRANBERRY-RASPBERRY SAUCE
2 to 3 cups fresh cranberries
1 cup orange juice
1 cup frozen raspberries
1 cinnamon stick
1 cup sugar

Soften the ice cream and mix in the remaining ingredients. Refreeze at least 8 hours.

For the sauce, cook the cranberries, cinnamon stick, and orange juice. Bring to a boil and simmer for 5 minutes. Add the raspberries and simmer 3 more minutes. Stir in the sugar. Serve hot or cold over the ice cream.

Yields 6 to 8 servings

The Checkerberry Inn
62644 County Road 37
Goshen, Indiana

Chèvre and Ginger Ice Cream

This ice cream is delicious served garnished with chopped, crystallized ginger. It's also wonderful served with pumpkin pie at Thanksgiving. Or by itself on the Fourth of July. Or anytime.

6 ounces fresh ginger root
7 cups heavy cream, divided
8 egg yolks
4 eggs
1¾ cups sugar
1 pound chèvre, preferably
  unsalted

Peel the ginger and dice fine. Place in a heavy-bottomed saucepan with 5 cups of the cream. Scald the cream.

In a mixing bowl, mix together the egg yolks, whole eggs, and sugar, beating until well combined. Using a whisk, slowly add the hot cream-and-ginger mixture into the eggs until completely combined. Remove the chèvre from the refrigerator and allow to come to room temperature.

Meanwhile, pour the egg-and-cream mixture back into the same heavy-bottomed saucepan and place over low heat. Stir constantly until the mixture reaches 185 degrees or until it coats the back of a spoon. This will take some time, about 30 to 45 minutes. Be careful not to overcook or it will curdle.

Strain the cream to remove the bits of ginger root. In a mixing bowl, slowly whisk together the chèvre with the egg custard. For the best results, add the custard a bit at a time to the chèvre, slowly adding a bit more custard as each addition becomes incorporated.

When totally incorporated, stir in the remaining 2 cups of cream and refrigerate at least 6 hours before churning. Freeze following the ice cream maker's instructions.
Yields 1 gallon

L'Etoile
25 North Pinckney Street
Madison, Wisconsin

Melon Granite

4 pounds melon pulp
  (cantaloupe, honeydew, etc.)
2 cups fresh lemon juice
12 to 16 ounces honey,
  depending on sweetness of
  melons
10 ounces Cointreau

Peel and seed the melons. Weigh the cleaned pulp. Puree in a food processor or blender until no lumps are visible. Add all other ingredients to taste.

Place a small amount of the mixture in the freezer to test consistency. Test when it is completely frozen. If it's too soft, add more fruit pulp. If it's too hard, add either more Cointreau or honey (or both) and test again.

To complete, either freeze in an ice cream machine or pour into a stainless steel pan and freeze in the freezer. When frozen, mix to a uniform consistency and transfer to a container.

The Golden Mushroom
18100 West Ten Mile Road
Southfield, Michigan

America Bowman Pie

Missouri is a major pecan producer and here's a local version of one of America's favorite desserts.

4 eggs
1 cup sugar
1 cup light corn syrup
1 cup butter, melted
1 teaspoon vanilla extract
1 dash of salt
1½ cups chopped pecans
1½ cups semisweet chocolate
  morsels
1 10-inch pastry shell, unbaked
Heavy cream, whipped

Preheat the oven to 375 degrees. Beat the eggs with a whisk. Beat in the sugar, corn syrup, butter, vanilla, and salt. Beat well. Stir in the pecans and chocolate morsels. Pour the filling into the unbaked pastry shell. Set the pie on a cookie sheet. Place the cookie sheet in the oven and bake for 15 minutes. Lower the temperature to 350 degrees and bake for another 35 to 40 minutes. Serve warm with the whipped cream.

America Bowman Keeping Room
Short Street at Welt
Weston, Missouri

Apple Cider Tart

PASTRY
6 ounces unsalted butter
3 cups unbleached flour
1 teaspoon salt
1/4 cup sugar
2 egg yolks
7 to 8 tablespoons heavy cream

FILLING
3 cups fresh apple cider
1 cup maple sugar or packed
    light brown sugar
4 eggs
2 egg yolks
4 tablespoons unsalted butter
1/2 teaspoon nutmeg

TOPPING
4 tablespoons butter
1/3 cup maple sugar or light
    brown sugar
3 firm apples, peeled, cored, and
    thinly sliced

GARNISH
1/2 cup slightly sweetened
    whipped cream
Sour cream to taste
Nutmeg to taste

For the pastry, cut the butter into 1/2-inch pieces and place in the bowl of a food processor. Add the flour, salt, and sugar. Process only until combined but still coarse-textured. Add the 2 egg yolks and cream and process until the dough starts to come together. Remove to a board and quickly knead the dough into a flat round. Wrap in plastic wrap and chill for at least 1 hour.

Preheat the oven to 350 degrees. On a lightly floured surface, roll the dough out to about 1/8-inch thickness and use it to line 8 4½-inch tart pans. Line the pastry with foil, add pie weights or dried beans, and bake until the pastry edges are slightly colored, about 15 minutes. Remove from the oven, leaving the oven on.

For the filling, pour the cider into a nonreactive saucepan. Cook over high heat until reduced by half, 10 to 15 minutes. Add 1 cup maple sugar and stir until dissolved. Beat the eggs and egg yolks in a bowl. Gradually pour the hot cider syrup over them, stirring continuously. Stir in the butter and nutmeg. Pour this filling into the tart shells.

Bake the tarts at 350 degrees until the filling just sets, 15 to 20 minutes. For the topping, heat the butter in a saute pan. Stir in the sugar until dissolved. Add the apple slices and cook them just until wilted. Arrange the slices on top of the tarts. This recipe may be prepared ahead to this point.

Heat the broiler. Place the tarts under the broiler until the apples start to caramelize. Serve warm or at room temperature with slightly sweetened whipped cream mixed to taste with sour cream. Grate nutmeg over the cream.

Tapawingo
9502 Lake Street
Ellsworth, Michigan

Apple Pie with Shaker Crumb Topping

1 9-inch pie shell
3 cups apples, peeled, cored, and
    sliced
1 cup sugar
¼ teaspoon nutmeg
¼ teaspoon cinnamon
⅓ cup flour

TOPPING
½ cup butter
½ cup brown sugar
1 cup flour

Preheat the oven to 350 degrees. Place the apples in the pie shell. Sprinkle with the sugar, nutmeg, cinnamon, and flour.

Melt the butter in a small saucepan and mix in the flour and brown sugar. The mixture should resemble coarse crumbs.

Top the pie with this mixture and bake for approximately 30 minutes.

The Golden Lamb
227 South Broadway
Lebanon, Ohio

Bayfield Maple and Walnut Pie

T his recipe makes three pies. If you think that's excessive, you haven't tasted Bayfield Maple and Walnut Pie. Give a party and cement some friendships.

3 9-inch pie shells, unbaked
1 cup melted butter
2 teaspoons salt
12 eggs, beaten
2 cups sugar
4 cups 100% maple syrup
4 cups chopped walnuts

Preheat the oven to 350 degrees. Mix all ingredients except the nuts together to form a smooth batter. Add the nuts and pour into the pie shells. Bake until the filling is set, about 45 minutes. Cool and serve with maple ice cream or a premium vanilla ice cream. This would also be good served with crème fraîche.

The Old Rittenhouse Inn
Bayfield, Wisconsin

Raisin Cream Pie

Carroll Marshall claims he's a "damn good piemaker." This recipe was his mother's. He tinkered with it and brought it to its present perfection. He claims for success you must balance the sugar with salt and that's why he always includes a quarter teaspoon of salt in all his pies.

Baked pastry shell for 1 10-inch
    deep dish pie

FILLING
1 cup raisins
Water to cover
1 cup sugar
1/2 cup flour
1/4 teaspoon salt
1 cup heavy cream
1/2 cup milk
4 egg yolks
1 tablespoon butter, melted
1 teaspoon vanilla extract

MERINGUE
4 egg whites
1/2 teaspoon cream of tartar
1 pinch of salt
1/2 cup sugar

Preheat oven to 350 degrees. For the filling, place the raisins in a saucepan and barely cover with water. Cook over medium heat just until tender and plumped. Drain the raisins, reserving the liquid. In a measuring cup, pour in 1 cup of raisin liquid.

In a heavy-bottomed saucepan, combine the sugar, flour, and salt. Gradually stir in the cream, reserved raisin liquid, and milk. Cook and stir until thickened and bubbly. Reduce the heat and cook and stir for 2 minutes more. In a medium bowl, lightly beat the egg yolks. Gradually stir about 1 cup of the hot mixture into the egg yolks and immediately return the egg yolks to the mixture in the saucepan and bring to a gentle boil. Cook and stir for 2 minutes more. Remove from heat and add the butter and vanilla. Fold in the raisins. Let cool slightly.

For the meringue, in a large bowl with an electric mixer, beat the egg whites with the cream of tartar and salt until frothy. Gradually add sugar and beat until stiff but not dry peaks form. Spread over the pie as directed. This makes enough meringue for a 10-inch pie.

Pour filling into the pie shell, spread with meringue, and bake for 12 to 15 minutes. Cool to room temperature and then cover and refrigerate.

Yields 8 servings

The White Way
Durant, Iowa

Cranberry and Almond Meringue Tart

1 10-inch fluted removable-
    bottom tart pan

CRUST
2 ounces sugar
4 ounces butter
1 egg
5 ounces sifted flour
3 ounces ground toasted almonds

CRANBERRY MERINGUE FILLING
1/2 cup egg whites
1 pinch salt
1/2 teaspoon cream of tartar
1 ounce sugar
3 ounces confectioner's sugar
12 ounces cranberries
4 ounces ground toasted almonds
2 tablespoons flour

GLAZED CRANBERRIES
1 cup sugar
4 to 5 ounces cranberries, rinsed
    and drained
1/2 cup water

For the crust, have all ingredients at room temperature. Using a mixer with a paddle, cream the sugar and butter at medium speed about 2 minutes or until light and fluffy. Scrape down the bowl and add the egg and mix until emulsified. Scrape down the bowl and add the flour and almonds, which you have mixed together. Mix slowly until the dough just comes together. The dough will be moist. Press the dough into the tart shell, making sure it is of even thickness. Use some flour on your hands as you are pressing it in. Place the dough in the freezer for at least 30 minutes.

Preheat the oven to 400 degrees. Place a sheet of aluminum foil filled with dry beans or other weight in the pie shell and bake for 6 minutes. Remove the foil and bake for 6 more minutes. If the dough puffs up in the middle, simply push it down gently with a towel. Let the shell cool on a cake rack. Do not remove from the tart pan.

Preheat the oven to 350 degrees. Place the egg whites, salt, and cream of tartar in a mixer with a whip. Whip at medium speed until frothy. Add the sugar, continue whipping until soft peaks form, and then add the confectioner's sugar and continue whipping until stiff peaks form. Be careful not to over-whip—the peaks should be stiff but not dry.

In another bowl, mix the cranberries, which have been rinsed and drained, with the almonds and flour. Fold this mixture into the meringue and place into the tart shell. Use a palate knife to smooth out the top and mound it slightly in the center. Place in the preheated oven and bake for 15 to 20 minutes. Turn off the oven but do not open the door. Leave in the oven for at least 2 hours or until the oven cools.

Remove from the tart pan and garnish with the glazed cranberries. Dust the edge with confectioner's sugar. Do not refrigerate.

The glazed cranberries may be prepared ahead by simply dissolving the sugar in water and bringing to a boil. Pour over the cranberries in a bowl and let sit overnight.

Sanford
1547 North Jackson Street
Milwaukee, Wisconsin

Rhubarb Pie

CRUST
2 cups sifted flour
⅓ cup confectioner's sugar
½ cup chilled butter

FILLING
2 eggs
1½ cups sugar
¼ cup flour
¾ teaspoon salt
1 tablespoon cinnamon
3 cups rhubarb, cut into ¼-inch
 pieces

Preheat the oven to 350 degrees. For the crust, sift the flour and confectioner's sugar together. Add the butter and cut into the flour mixture until well blended. The quickest way to do this is in a food processor fitted with a metal blade. Or you can use a pastry blender or 2 knives.

Pat the mixture into a 10-inch springform pan. Prebake in the preheated oven for 15 minutes.

Beat the eggs with the sugar, adding in the flour, salt, and cinnamon until all are well blended. Fold in the rhubarb and put the filling into the crust. Bake until set, about 45 to 50 minutes. Serve warm.

Yields 8 servings

Prairie Restaurant
500 South Dearborn
Chicago, Illinois

Chocolate Steamed Pudding with Ellie's Mom's Sauce

Here's a recipe that exemplifies the best of the traditional. "Ellie's Mom" is Quivey's executive chef Craig Kuenning's grandmother. This dessert is one of the restaurant's most popular—try it and you'll see why.

PUDDING
1 tablespoon butter
1½ ounces unsweetened chocolate
1 egg
½ teaspoon vanilla extract
1 cup coffee, cooled
1½ cups flour, sifted
¼ teaspoon salt
1½ teaspoons baking powder

SAUCE
2½ cups sifted confectioner's sugar
2 eggs
¼ pound plus 2 tablespoons butter
¼ teaspoon salt
1½ teaspoons vanilla extract
1 cup heavy cream

Preheat the oven to 350 degrees. Butter 8 6-ounce custard cups. For the pudding, in a double boiler over very low heat, melt the butter and chocolate. Set aside to cool.

Beat the eggs and sugar together. Add the vanilla and beat again. Add the chocolate mixture and mix again. Add the cooled coffee and blend well. Sift the dry ingredients together and add. The batter should be smooth. Using a 4-ounce ladle, fill the custard cups with the chocolate mixture. Cover each cup tightly with aluminum foil.

Set the cups in a deep baking pan and add ½ inch of hot water to the pan. Cover the pan with foil and put into the oven. Steam for 30 minutes. Cool slightly before unmolding. Serve warm with Ellie's Mom's Sauce.

Yields 8 servings

For the sauce, chill a large mixing bowl and whisk in the freezer.

Combine the confectioner's sugar, eggs, butter, salt, and vanilla in another bowl and beat until creamy and smooth.

Put the heavy cream into the chilled bowl and beat until slightly thickened. Continue to beat with the chilled whisk and slowly fold in the egg mixture, maintaining as much air as possible in the cream. Whip by hand until smooth.

Yields 3 cups

Quivey's Grove
6261 Nesbit Road
Madison, Wisconsin

Maple Rice Pudding

1½ cups long grain rice
4 cups milk
1 teaspoon vanilla extract
3 egg yolks
¼ cup superfine sugar
2 tablespoons unflavored gelatin
1 tablespoon lemon juice
1 tablespoon water
½ cup finely chopped candied
    fruit
¾ cup 100% maple syrup
2 egg whites
1 cup heavy cream, whipped

Place the rice, 3½ cups of the milk, and the vanilla in a heavy-bottomed saucepan and cook over low heat, stirring occasionally, until all the milk is absorbed. Continue to stir and add small amounts of the remaining ½ cup of milk until the rice is soft.

Beat the egg yolks and sugar until pale yellow. Dissolve the gelatin in the lemon juice and water over low heat. Add to the egg mixture.

Place the rice, egg mixture, maple syrup, and candied fruit in a large bowl over another bowl full of crushed ice. Stir together until cool.

Whip the egg whites to hold a soft shape and then fold into the mixture. Fold in the whipped cream. Spoon into serving dishes and refrigerate at least 1 hour.

Yields 6 servings

Public Landing Restaurant
200 West 8th Street
Lockport, Illinois

Warm Persimmon Pudding with Dried Blueberries

5 tablespoons unsalted butter
1 large persimmon or 1 cup
    persimmon puree
2 eggs
¾ cup firmly packed brown
    sugar
¾ cup flour
½ teaspoon baking powder
½ teaspoon baking soda
¼ teaspoon salt
2 teaspoons cinnamon
1 teaspoon ginger
½ teaspoon nutmeg
¼ teaspoon cloves
1 cup half and half
¼ cup dried blueberries
1 cup heavy cream (optional)
1 tablespoon confectioner's sugar
    (optional)

Buttered ramekins or custard
    cups

Preheat the oven to 350 degrees. Coat the insides of 8 ½-cup ramekins with 1 tablespoon of the butter. Halve the persimmon lengthwise, scrape the flesh into the work bowl of a food processor fitted with a metal blade, and puree.

Measure 1 cup of the persimmon puree into a large bowl, discarding or reserving the remaining puree for another use.

Mix the puree with the eggs and brown sugar and set aside.

Sift the dry ingredients together. Melt the remaining 4 tablespoons butter and mix with the half and half.

Stir in the dry ingredients and butter alternately into the puree. Stir in the blueberries. Divide the mixture evenly between the buttered ramekins.

Adjust the oven rack to the middle setting. Put the ramekins on a baking sheet and bake until the puddings are set and a knife inserted comes out clean, 30 to 35 minutes. Cool 10 minutes. If desired, whip the cream with the sugar to soft peaks and top the puddings with a dollop of cream and sprinkled confectioner's sugar.

Yields 8 servings

Prairie Restaurant
500 South Dearborn
Chicago, Illinois

Green Grape Bread Pudding

6 slices bread
1½ cups green grapes
2½ cups milk
2½ tablespoons butter, melted
⅓ cup sugar
2 teaspoons brandy extract
3 eggs, beaten
Zest of 1 lemon
¼ teaspoon cinnamon
¼ teaspoon vanilla extract

Preheat the oven to 375 degrees. Butter a 1½-quart baking dish.

Cut the crusts off the bread slices, cut each slice into 9 squares, and place them in the buttered baking dish. Remove the grapes from the stems, wash, and dry. Add to the bread squares and toss.

In a large mixing bowl, beat together the milk, butter, sugar, eggs, lemon zest, brandy extract, cinnamon, and vanilla. Pour over the bread-and-grape mixture. Bake for about 45 minutes or until golden brown. Serve warm or cold with softly whipped cream.

Yields 6 to 8 servings

The Hannah Marie Country Inn
Highway 71 South
Spencer, Iowa

Fresh Rhubarb Strudel with Rhubarb Sauce and Rhubarb Ice

STRUDEL
1½ pounds diced rhubarb
1½ cups sugar
½ cup flour
2 teaspoons cinnamon
½ teaspoon nutmeg
¼ teaspoon cloves
½ cup chopped walnuts
6 filo dough leaves
½ pound melted butter
½ cup bread crumbs
Powdered red food coloring
   (optional)

SAUCE
1 pound rhubarb, diced
1 cup sugar
1 cup water
1 pinch each of cinnamon and
   salt
1 tablespoon fresh lemon juice
Powdered red food coloring
   (optional)

ICE
2 pounds diced rhubarb
1 cup sugar
1 cup water
1 pinch cinnamon
1 egg white
2 ounces Cognac
1 cup dry Champagne
Powdered red food coloring
   (optional)

Rotating ice cream maker

For the strudel, preheat the oven to 425 degrees and butter a baking tray. If desired sprinkle the rhubarb with the red food coloring and mix. Use just enough to obtain a rosy glow. Add the sugar, flour, spices, and nuts. Mix. Add 2 tablespoons melted butter and again mix.

Lay one sheet of filo dough in front of you on a double sheet of waxed paper. Sprinkle dough generously with butter, then with bread crumbs. Repeat with the remaining leaves of dough, stacking one on top of another. Sprinkle the top extra generously with butter and crumbs.

Pile the rhubarb filling along the edge closest to you, and then with the aid of the waxed paper, roll tightly away from you, leaving approximately 1½ inches unrolled. Carefully pick up the strudel, with the help of the paper, and turn out onto the buttered baking tray, completing the rolling of the strudel in the process, leaving the seam side down on the tray. Brush the outside of the strudel with butter and bake for approximately 30 minutes, basting with the remaining butter every 10 minutes.

For the sauce, combine all the ingredients except the lemon juice in a saucepan. Bring to a boil and cook over medium heat for approximately 15 minutes or until the rhubarb mixture is a syrupy consistency. Adjust the coloring if necessary and add the lemon juice to taste. The amount of both depends on the natural color of the rhubarb and the degree of sweetness desired. Puree in a blender, cool to room temperature, and refrigerate.

For the ice, place the rhubarb, sugar, and water in a saucepan and cook over medium heat for about 15 minutes. Remove the cooked rhubarb from the liquid and reserve. To the rhubarb liquid, add a pinch of cinnamon and food coloring if desired and then reduce the liquid to 1½ cups.

Puree the reserved rhubarb with the reduced syrup. Add the egg white and blend again. Add the Cognac and chill. Once chilled, blend in the Champagne and freeze in a rotating ice cream maker.

Serve the strudel warm with the sauce at room temperature and the rhubarb ice.

The Cottage
525 Torrence Avenue
Calumet City, Illinois

SAUCES, SEASONINGS, AND SPECIALTIES

This chapter includes a lot of different things, a sort of culinary catchall. The recipes include everything from Dried Cherry Truffles to Mom's Easy Popcorn Balls. (Since two states in the Midwest both claim to produce the world's best popcorn, at least one recipe had to use popcorn!)

There are also glazes for meat, preserves and marmalades, and other imaginative ideas that didn't fit any other category, but deserved inclusion in this book.

Apple Cider Sauce

Try this sauce with the inn's Gingerbread Waffles (see the recipes for Brunch).

2 cups apple cider
2 tablespoons cornstarch
½ cup sugar
½ cup butter
1½ cups light corn syrup
Juice and zest of 2 lemons
½ teaspoon nutmeg
¼ teaspoon ginger

Dissolve the cornstarch in a little of the apple cider.

Mix all the ingredients together in a large saucepan. Cook over medium heat until thickened, stirring constantly.

Serve warm over pancakes, waffles, ice cream, apple dumplings, and apple, pumpkin, or mince pie.

Yields about 3 cups sauce

The Apple Orchard Inn
Missouri Valley, Iowa

Aunt Clara's Strawberry Preserves

This recipe was given to innkeeper Bev Meyer by her Aunt Clara. At the Evergreen it's served on homemade bread.

2 cups strawberries, crushed
2 cups strawberries, whole
4 cups sugar

Jelly jars
Paraffin or lids and bands

Put the crushed strawberries and 2 cups of the sugar in a heavy-bottomed saucepan. Bring to a boil, stirring to dissolve the sugar. Boil for 10 minutes, stirring occasionally to prevent scorching.

Add the whole strawberries and the remaining sugar. Boil the mixture for another 10 minutes, stirring occasionally.

Pour into a large bowl to cool and stir often. The faster the steam is released, the thicker the preserves will be. Let stand for 24 hours before putting the preserves into sterilized jars and sealing with wax or processing in a hot-water bath.

Yields 5 8-ounce jars

Evergreen Knoll Acres
Lake City, Minnesota

Peach-Orange Marmalade

Michigan is a major peach producer. This recipe takes advantage of that. Although it's a time-consuming recipe, innkeeper Gloria Krys says opening a jar on a cold February morning brings the color and flavor of summer to the table.

20 medium peaches (Red Havens are best)
10 cups sugar
6 oranges

Canning jars, pints
Caps and bands

Scald, peel, and dice the peaches. Squeeze the juice from the oranges. Remove the membrane from the inner peel of the oranges and process the peels in a food processor or grinder until they're in small pieces, or chop finely with a knife.

Combine all the ingredients in a large ceramic or stainless steel bowl. Cover and let stand overnight.

Put the uncooked marmalade in a large, heavy-bottomed saucepan. Place the saucepan over medium heat, stirring until the sugar dissolves completely. Bring to a boil and cook over moderate heat until clear and thick, about 1 hour. Stir frequently to prevent scorching.

Pour into hot, sterilized pint jars, leaving ¼-inch head space. Adjust caps and bands and process for 15 minutes in a boiling-water-bath canner.

Remove from the bath and let the jars cool in a draft-free place. When cooled, remove the bands, label the jars, and store.

The Urban Retreat
2759 Canterbury Road
Ann Arbor, Michigan

Maple-Cranberry Glaze

This glaze represents the best the northwoods has to offer—pure maple syrup and cranberries.

½ pound cranberries
1 cup 100% maple syrup
2 tablespoons butter
¾ cup sour cream or yogurt
   (optional)

Cook the ingredients together in a saucepan over medium heat until the cranberry skins pop open. Strain through a sieve and use as a glaze for meat.

This can also be adapted as a sauce for fresh fruit by adding ¾ cup sour cream or yogurt.

North Star Lodge
Star Lake, Wisconsin

Mom's Easy Popcorn Balls

1 cup brown sugar, packed
8 cups miniature marshmallows
1 stick butter
8 quarts freshly popped popcorn
   (2 tablespoons unpopped corn
   equals 4 cups popped corn)

Waxed paper
Food coloring (optional)

Place the freshly popped popcorn in a large bowl. In a heavy-bottomed saucepan over medium heat, melt the brown sugar, the marshmallows, and the butter, stirring to combine well.

Pour the mixture over the popcorn. Working quickly, butter your hands and form balls. Place on waxed paper until the balls are cool and no longer sticky. You may add food coloring to the butter mixture before pouring over the popcorn, if desired.

Bonaparte's Retreat
Bonaparte, Iowa

Dried Cherry Truffles

6 tablespoons heavy cream
2 tablespoons unsalted butter
6 ounces semisweet chocolate
1 teaspoon almond extract
1/3 cup dried cherries
1 1/2 tablespoons Amaretto
Sifted unsweetened cocoa
   powder

COATING
1 pound semisweet chocolate,
   finely chopped
1 square inch paraffin, finely
   chopped

Round toothpicks
Waxed paper
Melon baller

Bring the cream and the butter to a simmer in a small, heavy-bottomed saucepan over medium heat, stirring frequently. Reduce the heat to low and add the 6 ounces of semisweet chocolate. Whisk until smooth. Pour into a bowl and add the almond extract. Combine the dried cherries and Amaretto and then add this mixture to the warm chocolate. Stir once or twice as the mixture cools. Refrigerate overnight or until firm enough to hold a shape.

Line a baking sheet with waxed paper. Dust generously with cocoa powder. Scoop the truffle mixture with a melon baller, using about 1 1/2 tablespoons per scoop. Roll each ball in the sifted cocoa powder and shape into a smooth round by rolling between the palms of your hands. Place on the waxed paper–lined baking sheet. When all the mixture has been shaped, cover with plastic wrap and freeze the truffles until ready to dip.

In a double boiler, first melt the paraffin over very hot water and then add the chopped chocolate. Stir until the chocolate is melted and its temperature reaches 115 to 120 degrees. Remove from the heat. Using round toothpicks stuck into each truffle, dip each into the melted chocolate, coating the truffle completely. Return the dipped truffles to the waxed paper to cool, removing the toothpicks. Store the cooled truffles in a tightly covered container and keep refrigerated.

Yields 12 truffles

The Rowe Inn
County Road C48
Ellsworth, Michigan

Inns and Restaurants

The designation "B&B" after the name in a listing indicates a bed and breakfast establishment. The page numbers after the name refer to the recipes from that establishment.

ILLINOIS

Charlie Trotter's   *94, 125*
816 West Armitage Street
Chicago, Illinois
312/248–6228
All major credit cards
Reservations necessary

Cindi's Cafe and Catering   *75*
222 South 9th Street
Mount Vernon, Illinois
618/242–6221
No credit cards
No reservations

The Cottage   *138*
525 Torrence Avenue
Calumet City, Illinois
312/891–3900
Credit cards: V, MC
Reservations requested

Eagle Ridge Inn and Resort   *86*
Highway 20 East
Galena, Illinois
815/777–2444
Credit cards: V, MC
Reservations recommended

Elsah's Landing Restaurant   *18, 45*
18 La Salle Street
Elsah, Illinois
618/374–1607
No credit cards
Reservations for luncheon
   and tea only

Foley's   *17, 77, 95*
211 East Ohio Street
Chicago, Illinois
312/645–1261
All major credit cards
Reservations advised

Le Français   *124*
269 South Milwaukee Street
Wheeling, Illinois
312/541–7470
All major credit cards
Reservations necessary

Maldaner's   *38*
222 South Sixth Street
Springfield, Illinois
217/522–4313
Credit cards: V, MC
Reservations accepted

Prairie Restaurant   *37, 47, 82*
500 South Dearborn   *133, 136*
Chicago, Illinois
312/663–1143
All major credit cards
Reservations advisable for
   dinner

Printer's Row   *112*
550 South Dearborn
Chicago, Illinois
312/461–0780
All major credit cards
Reservations advisable

OHIO

The Apple Farm Restaurant   *65*
262 Pearl Road
Brunswick, Ohio
216/225–5576
All major credit cards
No reservations

Arnold's Bar and Grill   *56, 102*
210 East Eighth Street
Cincinnati, Ohio
513/421–6234
No credit cards
Reservations suggested for
   six or more

L'Auberge   *33*
4120 Far Hills Avenue
Dayton, Ohio
513/299–5536
Credit cards: V, MC, AE
Reservations suggested

The Baricelli Inn   *116*
2203 Cornell Road
Cleveland, Ohio
216/791–6500
Credit cards: V, MC, AE
Reservations necessary

Betsey Mills Dining Room   *4*
300 4th Street
Marietta, Ohio
614/373–3804
Credit Cards: V, MC
No reservations

The Chadwick Inn   *21, 52*
301 River Road
Maumee, Ohio
419/893–2388
Credit cards: V, MC
No reservations

The Golden Lamb   *64, 130*
227 South Broadway
Lebanon, Ohio
513/932–5065
All major credit cards
Reservations advisable

The Heritage Restaurant   *73*
7664 Wooster Pike
Cincinnati, Ohio
513/561–9300
Credit cards: V, MC, AE
Reservations suggested

Hulbert's Restaurant   *5*
1033 Bridge Street
Ashtabula, Ohio
216/964–2594
No credit cards
No reservations

Lock 24 Restaurant   *106*
State Route 154
Elkton, Ohio
216/424–3710
Credit cards: V, MC
No reservations

Peerless Mill Inn   *46*
319 South Second Street
Miamisburg, Ohio
513/866–5968
Credit cards: V, MC, AE
No reservations

The Phoenix   *62*
30 Garfield Place
Cincinnati, Ohio
513/721–2255
All major credit cards
Reservations requested

Rigsby's Cuisine Volatile   *103*
692 North High Street
Columbus, Ohio
614/461–7888
Credit cards: V, MC, AE
Reservations recommended

Ristorante Giovanni   *71, 114, 122*
25550 Chagrin Boulevard
Cleveland, Ohio
216/831–8626
Credit cards: V, MC, AE
Reservations suggested

Sammy's   *61, 88, 98*
1400 West 10th Street
Cleveland, Ohio
216/523–5560
All major credit cards
Reservations suggested

 # *Recommended Reading*

These books represent a look at American cooking in general and several offer a particular look at certain aspects. All are good reading and all, except the *Interstate Gourmet*, contain recipes.

American Cookery   James Beard   Little, Brown and Company, 1972
One of the best collections of American recipes with Mr. Beard's invaluable commentary.

The American Heritage Cookbook   Editors of American Heritage with Evan Jones, Cleveland Amory, Lucius Beebe, etc.   American Heritage Publishing Co. Inc., 1964
For the history of eating and drinking in America, this one can't be beaten. Interesting traditional recipes.

An American Folklife Cookbook   Joan Nathan   Schocken Books, 1984
A good look around the country at cooking folkways that are dying out.

I Hear America Cooking   Betty Fussell   Elisabeth Sifton-Viking Press, 1986
A survey of regional cooking, interesting recipes.

The Interstate Gourmet: Midwest   Neal O. Weiner and David Schwartz   Summit Books/Simon and Schuster, 1986
While the authors disclaim responsibility because of the volatility of the restaurant business, this is a must-have book for any traveler.

The Flavor of Wisconsin   Harva Hachten   State Historical Society of Wisconsin Press, 1981
Ms. Hachten has done for Wisconsin what the editors of American Heritage did for the country as a whole.

A Cook's Tour of Iowa   Susan Puckett   University of Iowa Press, 1988
A fascinating look at one state's culinary heritage with recipes, good ones.

 *Index*

Entries in capital letters indicate chapter titles.

Born in the Midwest but raised on the East Coast, Margaret Guthrie moved back to the Midwest with the Bicentennial in 1976. Educated at Springside School and Brown University, she now lives in Madison, Wisconsin. She is the author of a series of cookbooks based on recipes from inns and restaurants of the individual states of the Midwest.